The Roads Taken: Complex Lives of Employed and At-Home Mothers

By

Deborah A. Kahn

Library of Congress Cataloging-in-Publication Data

Deborah A. Kahn, The Roads Taken: Complex Lives of Employed and At-Home Mothers, parenting, women, work-life balance

Summary: Research findings about at-home and employed mothers: choices, reasons, values, and consequences

ISBN: 978-1-939282-31-6

Published by Miniver Press, LLC, McLean Virginia

Copyright 2014 Deborah A. Kahn

All rights reserved under International and Pan-American Copyright Conventions. By payment of the required fees, you have been granted the non-exclusive, non-transferable right to access and read the text of this e-book on-screen. No part of this text may be reproduced, transmitted, down-loaded, decompiled, reverse engineered, or stored in or introduced into any information storage and retrieval system, in any form or by any means, whether electronic or mechanical, now known or hereinafter invented, without the express written permission of Nell Minow. For information regarding permission, write to editor@miniverpress.com

First edition May 2014

Dedication

To my husband, Harris, for being my backbone

and providing humor to

and unwavering support for my efforts

and

my adult children, Derek and Alexis, who I claim were easy and

wonderful

when they were growing up

and who claim my memory is faulty

The Roads Taken: Complex Lives of Employed And At-Home Mothers

Foreword by Janet C. Heddesheimer, Ph.D. 1

Introduction 5

1 - What *Should* I Do? 17
2 - What Do I Tell My Daughters? 36
3 - Is There An Ideal Work Status? 47
4 - What Is Parenting Anyway? 70
5 - What Are The Side Effects Of My Work Status? 92
6 - Why Do Mothers Change Their Work Status—Or Not? 114
7 - What Are The Challenges? 125
8 - Can We Really Have It All? 145
9 - Who Gives Us Support? 164
10 - Are The Gloves Off Yet? 181
11 - Where Do We Go From Here? 207

Appendix 225

Acknowledgments 257

Bibliography 261

The Road Not Taken

By Robert Frost

Two roads diverged in a yellow wood,
And sorry I could not travel both
And be one traveler, long I stood
And looked down one as far as I could
To where it bent in the undergrowth;

Then took the other, as just as fair,
And having perhaps the better claim,
Because it was grassy and wanted wear;
Though as for that the passing there
Had worn them really about the same,

And both that morning equally lay
In leaves no step had trodden black.
Oh, I kept the first for another day!
Yet knowing how way leads on to way,
I doubted if I should ever come back.

I shall be telling this with a sigh
Somewhere ages and ages hence:
Two roads diverged in a wood, and I—
I took the one less traveled by,
And that has made all the difference.

Foreword

Deborah and I have known each other for thirty some years and, in many ways, traversed the same road in balancing our work, intellectual interests, and commitment to family.

We have children about the same age and during the time I was mentoring her dissertation research, I was having the same conversations with myself about employment/home benefits that the women in her study were articulating. The opportunity I had to learn from the participants in her research helped me to make thoughtful decisions about my own life and family. So for that I say thank you to Deborah for being my doctoral student and for continuing our friendship over time.

In the introduction to this important book, *The Roads Taken*, Deborah lays out quite nicely the journey she took in crafting the focus of her research. She notes, rightly so, that she struggled to find a topic for her dissertation and ultimately landed on what she cared about most—mothers and their work status decisions.

Deborah produced a stellar document that generated considerable discussion among the faculty. But she did not stop there. Remarkably, fourteen years later she did a follow-up study with the same group of women. I say remarkably because doctoral research rarely sustains itself beyond the research necessary to complete the degree.

What makes this conversation—remain employed or stay home debate—especially compelling is that, in part, women learn best from other women. They solve problems by asking other women how they navigate challenges and what they consider in deciding on a course of action. So Deborah made the centerpiece of her systematic study of employed and at-home mothers insights from the women who were walking that path.

In this follow-up study she asked the mothers about their work status changes and why or why not they had occurred; challenges they experienced; stresses related to their work status; and sources of support, wanting to learn how they guide their lives once children become part of their families. She recognized that such complicated matters become personally powerful when each woman is left to decide what is best for her.

Now those who read this book have access to the thoughts, views, feelings, and values of women who have made and/or changed their decisions over time about whether to stay at home or remain in the workplace. The takeaway here is that such matters are rarely resolved easily. While each woman makes her own decision it can now be an informed one based on the information shared by others who walked the path ahead of her.

Although the population in her research began with a select group (200) of mothers who had similar demographics, the content of *The Roads Taken* is actually relevant to all women and men too. The work covers life: challenges, stresses, support from family, effects of work status on life choices, handling health issues of family members. She presents and discusses situations we all experience; the degree of the situation may differ but the issues are comparable. Now we can take advantage of the diverse and honest thoughts of the women in her research group not only as they made decisions about employment or staying at home while growing their children to be responsible, productive adults in society but also, as they managed employment challenges, coped with declining health of parents, and aspired to personal fulfillment. Many of these events apply to all adults—women and men—whether they are married or not.

The Roads Taken provides considerable grist for discussion in many forums. Students in women's studies courses, members of book clubs, counselors, and parents or adults soon becoming a family will all find insightful information to bring to bear as they consider the same questions covered in Deborah's research. Unlike all too many of the books in this genre, which advocate a position, hers comes from a base of systematic data collection and analysis of responses and comments of full-, part-time employed, and at-home mothers. That gives added credibility to her probing, nonjudgmental questions and suggestions.

I take considerable pride in how she has sustained her quality research and focus these many years.

Janet C. Heddesheimer, Ph.D.
Professor Emeritus of Counseling
The George Washington University
Washington, D.C.

Introduction

I met Betty Friedan some 30 years after she published her groundbreaking book *The Feminine Mystique* (1963), which challenged the long-held notion that "a mother's place is in the home." I asked her what she thought of my being an at-home mother. Three times she did not hear my question but when she finally did, retorted, "Oh, I thought you said you were an asshole mother!" After clarifying my mothering competence and question, she suggested that "perhaps in time I would want to rejoin the workforce." Employment, in Freidan's eyes, afforded fulfillment. I wasn't so sure. Did she really mean fulfillment for all mothers?

Friedan's answer astonished and perplexed me. At the same time, I was immensely pleased because it confirmed to me that my dissertation topic—employed and at-home mothers—was indeed a subject worthy of study. My original research proposal had been on the effects of different drug treatment programs in prisons—quite a switch and another story—but of interest to me back in the 1970s and 80s when I had a career in the criminal justice system.

My journey of switching topics began on the day my first child was born. That also became my last one of employment for fourteen years and gave me another excuse not to write my dissertation still on the original topic. I had assumed I would be employed part time but had not really thought about the logistics. The funding was cut and so was my position. I did not have a passion for a career; my husband was financially and emotionally supportive. I became an at-home mother. I found, to my surprise, that I loved being at home with my children and I did not miss my position as Deputy Director of the National Coalition for Jail Reform.

But all was not bliss. I did not like the treatment I received from men *and* women. When I was at social gatherings with my husband, I would be talking with a small group feeling we were having an interesting and sometimes substantive discussion. In my mind we were all participating equally. However, when someone would ask me what I did—meaning what important employment I had—the equality disappeared when I said that I was at home with my children. They completely lost interest—they dismissed me. Some literally turned their backs on me! I was hurt. I was furious. And I was confused. I thought I had demonstrated a degree of intelligence and shared interests. Why did I suddenly not count?

I still had not written my dissertation on the drug treatment topic and was an at-home mother of two when I became co-chair of the Fun Fair, the major fundraiser of the year for my children's elementary school. Preparing for the Fun Fair was a lot of logistical, bureaucratic, and organizational work but had nothing to do with the actual activities of the Fair; there were chair people for that and about 98 percent of them were at-home mothers. Despite outreach efforts to each of them, they never needed any help and "had everything under control." This made me nervous but I remained steadfast to my decision to delegate. When I walked around checking each room the evening before the Fair, I was blown away. In the "Plant Sale" room, plants were set on risers—each with a ribbon around it, a name, a price tag—the presentation was colorful, clean, organized, inviting, and beautiful. This was true for each of the 20-plus rooms of different activities. I had an epiphany: these women do not sit around eating bon-bons; they are competent, smart, and independent—like employed mothers. Are they really so different? Why, if given the choice, does one mother choose full-time employment and another choose to stay at home? I had a new topic for my dissertation.

In the summer of 1994 I found a partial answer. I wanted to determine if the research findings on employed and at-home mothers, which concluded that employed women tended to be goal oriented and non-employed women were inclined to be nurturing, would be confirmed with a more controlled/homogenous sample population. The participants in the earlier studies were often freshman psychology students who definitely had opinions but no reality testing about what work status they would hold as mothers. Other study populations were women of different ages, marital status, and work status who may or may not have had children. The impetus for my dissertation was to determine if mothers who were similar on specific criteria but who differed in their work status would still have different character traits—achiever versus nurturer.

My study population consisted of mothers who: 1) were 35 to 45 years old; 2) had an employed spouse living in the home; 3) had at least two children—one of preschool age or younger; and 4) chose their current full-time work status—employment outside the home or at home caring for their children—because that is who they were, not for financial reasons.

As a result of these strict criteria, the participants were very well educated and financially comfortable; hardly typical of most mothers dealing with the family/employment struggle. However, confirmation of the earlier results by this select population would, in fact, be representative of all mothers because the populations in the earlier research studies were diverse. The women had different marital statuses, employment statuses, number and ages of children. If my findings confirmed the results of the earlier studies then we could conclude that the character trait of a woman—any age, with or without children, married or single, employed or at-home—would coincide with her work status. Or, so I thought.

I sent two questionnaires to 97 employed and 103 at-home participants. The first questionnaire focused on character traits; the other focused on rewards derived from work—employment or caring for children. Character traits are socially acceptable masculine and feminine traits but more positively associated with one gender than another. For example, being aggressive is socially acceptable for both men and women but we all know that if a man is aggressive we typically think he is demonstrating good, strong character and a woman? Well, we know what she's called....

I completed my dissertation: "Employed and At-Home Mothers: A Comparison of Gender-Related Character Traits and Psychological Rewards Derived from Work," in 1995. I found a difference. First, the mother work status groups differed in the rewards they derived from "work." The employed mothers found that challenge, achievement, and recognition were rewards of employment and at-home mothers thought that helping others and having an impact on others were rewards for staying home growing the children. This makes sense given the different environments, opportunities and responsibilities of employment from those afforded at home with the children.

I found an intriguing difference in their description of their character traits that did confirm the findings in the earlier research studies. Employed mothers described themselves as independent, competitive, decisive, and confident. The at-home mothers described themselves as gentle, concerned about others, understanding, and helpful. Their descriptors match perfectly society's expectations about what character traits are best in a particular role. For example: What is a good employee? Answer: one who is competitive, decisive, and competent. Similarly, what is a "good" mother? Answer: one who is gentle, concerned about others, and understanding. Was that it? Did they have different character traits?

No, not unequivocally. According to voluntary comments they wrote on the questionnaires, the mothers were very aware of what behavior was expected in a particular role and described themselves accordingly. In fact, their comments demonstrate that they did not necessarily think of themselves as having the character traits best associated—according to society—with an employed person or one at-home. At-home mothers wrote beside several descriptors, "I would have answered this differently if I were still working." And next to the trait assessing degree of competitiveness—"not at all /very competitive"—one mother wrote, "I used to be when I was working." Similarly, this awareness about expected behavior in a particular situation came from the employed mothers too. One employed mother wrote next to the descriptor "cries easily/never cries," "Never at the office!" And several employed mothers wrote next to other character traits on the questionnaire: "Are you talking about my personal-self or my professional-self?" So, if the difference found wasn't really a difference, but actually an awareness of the socially preferred character traits of a particular role in society, then what was going on? I had another question. Why would a mother, *if* she had the choice, choose one role over the other?

After receiving my doctorate from George Washington University I had the opportunity to teach a course in human development at Northern Virginia Community College and then to be a part of a ten-year project on the effects of early child care on youth development at the National Institute of Child Health and Human Development (NICHD), a branch of the National Institutes of Health (NIH). Despite those interesting experiences, my question continued to nag at me. At the end of my time at NICHD I again began talking about the internal battle that mothers (not fathers, yet) have about employment versus staying at home with their children. I think it was when one senior scientist dismissed my curiosity by saying that it was no longer an issue, "all mothers sought employment," that I decided I had to do more research.

In 2008, I went back to the 200 mothers who participated in my dissertation study to find out how they made decisions regarding employment and how they fared caring for home and hearth. The response rate was extraordinary; over 60 percent of the original 200 participants—123 of the mothers—agreed to participate in my follow-up study. Fourteen years had gone by since my first contact with these mothers. Their toddlers were now teenagers or college students; the mothers were now at least in their 50s and some of their marriages had dissolved into divorce or ended in widowhood. I asked them about changes in their work status; support from family and society; challenges and stresses they experienced; and a myriad of other questions about being a mother, daughter, wife, career woman.

This time, I got my answer and more. When asked: "What was a guiding force when making your decision regarding your work status?" the mothers tended to divide into two groups. The employed mothers wrote about achievement and independence: "I need to have a sense of career accomplishment beyond motherhood." And "I have always been a hard-working, competent person. I have also been very independent..." The at-home mothers' comments focused on nurturing and caring: "Once my children were born, I knew in my soul that I had to be home with them." And "I couldn't work outside the home and raise these kids the way I envisaged."

The mothers had different passions, different priorities—not specifically different character traits—about what was most important to them. In addition, the mothers took into account how their current circumstances—finances, education, spouse's support, health of all family members—including their own parents, and plans for the future—impacted their priorities before finally asking themselves "what do I really care about—what makes me happy, feel good about myself? What are my priorities? What is best for me and my family?" The data and their comments revealed that a mother's work choice is a personal decision based on her assessment of her current situation and priorities that can and often do change over time. It would be presumptive and erroneous to conclude that mothers make work status decisions based on their character traits. Employed mothers are also nurturers and do care greatly about their children. At-home mothers do have a personal drive for achievement and recognition as a competent, interesting adult.

My findings also indicated that a mother's priorities and assessment of her circumstances is an individual experience, which is different for different people at various times and in diverse situations. And, given what may appear to be the same situation for mothers may well not result in the same work status decision because we are individuals and each of us comes with our own experiences, values, expectations and perceptions. We cannot know for sure all that goes into another's work status decision. From my study, and the rich, honest, and thoughtful comments of the mothers, it is clear that motherhood is hard and we are all—whether employed or at home—trying to do the very best we can.

This book presents the analyses and discussions that emerged from the data and comments of the mothers in my studies. And with that information, the book looks toward the future. I offer recommendations for society, employers/HR people, policymakers, and all mothers. The focus of my suggestions is to lessen the stresses a mother faces while growing her children to be happy and responsible adults. Another important focus is to help mothers continue to grow and to feel strong and proud of themselves as adult women.

Recommendations for employers are derived from the consistent complaint of employed mothers. They need support and time to attend to needs of family members. Flextime, the sharing of a job and the ability to work from home are positive and powerful office policies that greatly assist mothers in the balancing act. In addition, mothers need respect and support for times when unexpected—sickness, spousal travel, weather-driven cancellations—demands from the home front upset the established routine.   Recommendations for the mothers focus on articulating issues that interfere with a smooth-running household with perfect, brilliant, happy, healthy children. In short, real life. These issues emerge from the comments of the employed and at-home mothers as they worked to attend to the demands and needs of their family, career (this includes motherhood), and society while trying not to forget about themselves. Mothers will be able to think about their own situation and compare their responses with those of the mothers in the different work status groups in this study. The responses of the mothers to challenges they experienced coupled with an awareness of personal goals reveal their values.

Mothers struggling with balancing family/employment are guided to: 1) objectively assess their current life situation and future needs/expectations; and 2) identify what is important to them and how they can go about validating themselves, reinforcing their efforts toward addressing their priorities. When we consciously and carefully make a decision after examining the many facets that impact a decision, including one that as much as possible is in sync with our priorities, we feel more in control, competent and happy. Our energy will be used to further our efforts in all aspects of employment and family responsibilities rather than wasting it feeling frustrated and exhausted trying to make ourselves feel better.

And when we feel good about ourselves, we have energy and a positive attitude to reach out towards others and give of ourselves. In a mother's situation, she will have the energy to help each child grow to be the very best person cognitively, psychologically, socially, and physically, that s/he can be.

Given that the data for this book were collected in 2008 (six years ago at this writing), there have been some changes. More and more I hear from mothers with young children that their husbands are active in the home and with the care of the children. "He will do anything I ask him to do." In addition, I hear that the use of cell phones greatly increases an employed mother's ability to be in communication—be available—to her children while in the office or out of town. Think about the communication abilities offered by Skype and FaceTime. What has not changed is that Mother still seems to be the primary parent who anticipates health, education, developmental, or psychological issues. And, this wonderful technology also enables "the office" to contact mother 24/7.

I also noticed that many of the blogs and opinions that are being written on the topic of employed and at-home mothers focuses on the employment/home balance or imbalance and what can be done about that. Another topic is efforts of women to become CEOs while being mothers with children in the home. And dads are getting attention too. One issue is the emergence and experiences of stay-at-home dads who enable their wives to pursue their careers full-steam ahead with no worries about the care of home or hearth. Another dad discussion is the call from dads to have recognition as "working dads." According to some of them, they, like the employed mothers, are struggling to balance employment and home.

These changes and articles I have mentioned above are exciting and demonstrate that our society is beginning to grapple seriously with the issues, challenges, and stresses of parenthood and mixing parenthood with career aspirations. I do, however, notice that these recent discussions focus on the employed mother and efforts to balance employment and home. Where are the discussions about the demands on at-home mothers who cannot separate office from home? They work 24/7 without pay, without promotions, without rewards. And, they handle chores and development of the children as well as the well-being of each family member and the family unit. Perhaps if we had more discussion articulating all that is involved with raising a family—the physical and emotional demands—we could better understand the complete and complex challenges for parents, employed and at-home. Further, dads want to be included in discussions about the employment/home demands on them and they suggest using the term "working dads." This term as well as "working mothers" continues the erroneous social mantra that at-home mothers "do nothing." We all know that at-home mothers work and they work very hard. Acknowledging that men want to be included, why not just change the phrase from "working dad" to "employed dad" as I have purposefully and carefully done in this book—"employed mother," not the term "working mother." Employed and at-home mothers both work; they work very hard, and now, we are educating ourselves that employed dads and at-home dads work very hard. They too want a voice at the "table."

All these changes and new discussions are definitely material for another study, but so far the issues revealed in the chapters of this book are still relevant to mothers. Actually, most of the topics are relevant to all women. As I mentioned above in this *Introduction*, the results of my dissertation confirmed the early research on employed and at-home women. This means that because the populations in these early studies were diverse—women differed in age; marital status; number, even existence of children; ages of children and/or work status; the findings and discussions in this book are applicable to all women, not just those who are mothers and who are financially able to choose employment or to stay at home.

I also believe that to a great extent, the topics are relevant to men who may be dads or not, and two sub-populations: One is the group of women who choose career over family and the second is the gay and lesbian population who may or may not choose marriage and children. After all, if we think about it, many of the issues discussed are just part of life. For example: balancing career and personal life are challenges for everyone; stress from employment conditions and illness are stressful whether children are in the picture or not; and becoming part of the sandwich generation is again, something most of us will experience.

Although I have no hard data, I believe that the material is pertinent to everyone regardless of sexual orientation. Why would gender or sexual orientation change the stress, challenges, or side effects of one's work status? Why would we think that a wife of a wife and a husband of a husband would not also grapple with the experiences and pressures found in either work status? Of course they would. Differences in communication within couples can be as diverse between homosexual couples as they can be within heterosexual couples. I, at this time, can only conclude that questions and concerns brought to light in *The Roads Taken* are applicable to all women and men who care for home and hearth and the many who try to succeed in careers outside the home.

Deborah A. Kahn
February 2014

Chapter 1

What *Should* I Do?

Things to consider when deciding your work status (employment or stay-at-home)

"What should I do?" That is a question a mother asks herself when deciding whether or not to remain employed or to stay at home. First, the "should" only confuses the process. I strongly suggest you delete it from your vocabulary. Instead, consider two factors that play a role in helping you make your decision. One factor is your current circumstances and the second is your values. Both factors are important and, indeed, intertwined. A good question to ask yourself is: "Given my current circumstances in areas that impact my family—our finances, my education, my spouse's support, health of all family members—including grandparents, and plans for the future, what are my priorities? The other question to ask yourself is: "What is really important to me?"—not what should matter or matters to my mother—but "what do I really care about—what makes me happy, feel good about myself? What are my priorities?"

Identifying circumstances to consider is not a straightforward process because: 1) situations change and 2) what one mother thinks is important another may not, because people have different values. Let us look at a few common factors that show the impact of a change in circumstances on work status decisions. Most frequently mothers identify the family's finances and health as most important when considering their work status options.

Financial situations can change because of changes in your 1) work status; 2) partner's work status; 3) marital status; 4) investments—if you have any. Think of the housing and financial markets' crash in 2008 when people who were making a lot of money suddenly became unemployed and their net worth plummeted. Or, as an acquaintance of mine noted: "health insurance can abruptly become vital to your family."

When this friend's husband lost his job they were suddenly without health insurance. Although she was employed, the plan her employer offered was not really good for the whole family, so she and their children were insured on his policy. Once he lost his coverage, she had to scramble to find a job with better benefits, i.e., health insurance coverage. Her spouse might have had some unemployment insurance for the short term, which definitely would have helped their household financial situation, but not bring in the money he usually earned, and definitely not enough to pay for health insurance for the family.

We all know that a death or divorce immediately changes one's financial situation. And, if it is a divorce, all too often mothers end up with a lot less money and more responsibility for the children. Splitting families means less money for someone. Yes, there are many wonderful dads who are exes who contribute a great deal. There are, unfortunately, still many who do not. These comments below describe the effect changes in family finances can have on us mothers:

> As a single mother, I had no choice but to work if I was going to take care of my son. The child support I received wasn't enough to take care of both of us.

> After my divorce, I switched to full time for financial reasons and to increase my benefit package.

When any of the elements that influence our work status decisions, such as financial situations, change over time, we need to reassess our work status choices. This mother tried to be prepared for financial changes:

> I realized everyone needs to be able to support themselves after seeing my own parents' divorce and watching my mom become the main source of income in my house.

The next year, she, too, divorced and secured part-time and later full-time employment.

Another concern that affects work status decisions of mothers is the health of family members. Health issues are not simple; they are complex. There are three components: physical, emotional, and academic/performance health. The physical and emotional health can apply to the children, either parent or either set of in-laws. Any aberration from healthy can affect the time and energy a mother has that may influence her decision regarding her work status. The quotes below illustrate some of the different ways health issues can impact employment decisions:

> My husband traveled constantly, and my girls had health issues that required a parent.

> My battle with breast cancer has made going back to work difficult.

> My youngest child was diagnosed with cancer in 1995. ... The head of my department became hostile toward my retaining my position. ... I was demoted. ...settlement in exchange for my agreeing to resign. ... In the end I realized that the outside world can impose severe stresses, fair or not, that force a mother to martial her limited resources for her children. What little self-esteem and energy I had left I gave to my children.

> My mother has been ill several times. Both my mother- and father-in-law were each ill, then died. All three have taken time and emotional energy to deal with over the years.

Another aspect of health, the academic and psychological health of our children is also a prevalent concern. And as financial circumstances can impact our work status as well as change over time, so can the health issues:

> My son has inattentive ADD. I have read many books and articles that state that kids with ADD benefit from having a full-time at home parent. It gave me encouragement for my choice to be available to my children first.

> One of my sons is on medical leave from college, after effects of over-prescribed medications for depression and wrongly prescribed meds for ADHD (did not have it).

Our situations or circumstances are connected to our values. The financial security of the family is often a circumstance that is considered when considering employment, but the extent to which the finances impact the decision process may differ because people have different values. One mother may feel that her spouse earns enough to take care of the family and thus, she either does not consider finances as impacting her decision or she sees it as supporting her freedom to choose to be an employed or an at-home mother.

> (I) truly never felt there was any other decision. Being a very active volunteer at school and church truly fulfilled that need to get out and do something—sometimes more than I would have liked. But we were very fortunate to be able to allow me to stay at home quite comfortably on one income. My children are not so sure they will have the same luxury.

I had the luxury of staying home with my kids with the exception of some part time work. Most moms do not have this choice and I'm happy that I was able to make the choice to spend more time with my kids.

A different mother, given that same income, may feel that that amount is not enough to live the lifestyle she wishes to have or to be able to send her children to private schools or college:

> Having to earn more to live in the Washington DC area in a comfortable home and in a great neighborhood

> We have established a life style that requires me to work if we want to keep it.

For the mother quoted below, changing financial circumstances, or, I should say, her assessment of the family's finances—the needs of the children and her desire to pursue her career—all played a role in her work status decisions:

> Financial needs guided my decision to stay with a job that was too demanding longer than I should. Then, once my husband was able to support the family, I decided that my family needs were greater than our financial needs or my need to continue to pursue my career. Now, a combination of needing to get my mind

clicking again along with huge tuition bills and retirement has led me back to the workforce.

And again, for a third mother, what her spouse earns may be irrelevant to her because what is of primary importance to her is that she has her own money and is financially independent:

> Working part time or stop working altogether would most likely lead to a lower-level or lower-paying job. (It is) important to be financially independent, to stand on my own two feet to support and provide for myself and my children if all else fails. Life is unpredictable, and I believe every woman/man needs to be prepared to survive on their own.

Or, just knowing yourself ... what you need to do, what makes you feel good about yourself:

> I would be unhappy and restless if I didn't work and have work-related projects.

> I think I would have driven everyone (except the dog) crazy as a stay-at-home mom.

As you can see from the diverse quotes above, financial issues can impact your work status decision. What financial circumstances you choose to consider depends upon what you feel is important to your family, which involves what you value. No one of us is right; our values are personal and our decisions are our own—right for each of us, not for everyone.

While circumstances and values are intertwined, sometimes other conditions also influence the situation. For example, you are likely to select the employment situation that is most compatible with your abilities, education, and responsibilities; i.e., achievements that you have worked hard to put into place you want to utilize; not ignore. The following quotes—one from an at-home mother and the other from an employed mother exemplify this influence:

> Because I was in Early Childhood Education, I think I am more fulfilled at home than some other mothers. I have felt that I am using my education in teaching my own children to become good and productive people.

> I had spent three years earning an MBA at night and wanted to use it in my career.

However, sometimes what is important to you—your values—overrides utilization of your achievements:

> Because I wanted more time with my children, I spent three years working part time at a job, which did not fully utilize my skills and experience.

> I do not get …satisfaction at home. Maybe it is because I do not get all the visibility and recognition

at home that I get at work, or it could be that I simply find home life less intellectually stimulating.

And conditions at "the office" can become too much; they push against your priorities:

> I cannot push hard for a career growth that may result in more responsibility requiring more time at work, working on weekends, or overseas travel because I must carefully balance my career, and my role as mother and wife.

> I left a high level managerial position which was well paid and high stress, because it offered little flexibility and personal and communal rewards.

> I was a substance abuse counselor. Many of the jobs available in the area were fairly dangerous and I was no longer willing to be in those situations. Being a parent of young children changed the jobs I was willing to consider.

Once we identify which circumstances are important to us and our family with awareness that our values have impacted this selection, we make decisions about our work status by examining how what is important to us—our personal values—addresses these situational issues in a manner that is best for us and our family. When we make a decision, we have, what I call, made a "choice." Whether we decide to be employed full or part time; in an ideal job or one that pays "enough"; or stay at home, we have made a choice.

Being aware that we are always making a choice is critical. We then accept responsibility for what we are doing and at the same time, we can realize that we are able to make a different choice—make changes—to our current situation. Acknowledging that we have choices empowers us. We have the ability to try to ensure that we are happy with ourselves, our family, and our career whether we are at home or employed.

Feelings of empowerment brought by acknowledging choice in employment decisions and subsequent behaviors are absent in the quote below:

> If I only knew that I would be able to find and love my current employment, I would not have minded the years of stay-at-home status. I also never knew that I would fall so completely in love with my children. My daughters and I have a wonderful, close relationship. We are a very strong and happy family.

This mother's frustration about having to give up her employment because she felt she had to care for the children is a feeling many women have experienced. To leave a satisfying employment situation and venture into the unknown and amorphous life of a stay-at-home mother is very difficult. Some mothers, like this one, claim that they "have no choice."

The truth is, we have choices and are always making choices, all day every day. Some choices are minor and insignificant but others may have a strong impact on our lives and extend beyond ourselves and our families.

My study's findings suggest she did, in fact, have a choice. She did not really have to stay at home; she chose to stay home. It may not feel that way at the time, but, in fact, she did choose the stay-at-home option. I say she had a choice because there are other mothers, who given similar circumstances, would and did choose to continue working. (Remember, we make decisions based on our evaluation of our circumstances and personal values!) They might have found a nanny, mother-in-law, or a daycare program so they could remain employed full time *or* they might have found a part-time job *or* a less demanding work environment, or some other way to achieve the employment/work at home balance she desired. This mother chose to stop her career and take care of her family; she could have chosen to continue her career or find similar or less demanding employment.

While she probably did love her career and was very happily employed, after assessing the needs of her family she made the decision; she chose to stay at home with her children. Why? The answer is simple and fundamental, if not sometimes elusive. Her values and experience drove her decision to put her family first.

This mother's values and experiences are different from a mother who, under similar circumstances, chooses to continue employment. Given her family's current financial situation, health, education, her relationship with her husband, type of employment, she decided that giving up her employment to care for her children was the best choice for her and her family. In the final analysis, her values, circumstances, and experiences drove her decision regarding her employment status. She made a choice.

Is she a better person for choosing to be with her children than a mother who chooses to remain in the workforce? No, she just has different values, different drives, and different experiences. Does the mother who chooses to remain in the workforce love her children "less?" No. Absolutely not. People are different and their choices may be different but one is not better than the other. What is different is that they perceive their needs differently as well as their experiences and priority of their values.

An example of values and how they affect experience, choice, and behavior is in this true, simplistic scenario from my own life. We have two dogs; one has just been let inside from being on wet ground and has filthy paws, the second dog has thrown up, leaving several piles of who knows what on the kitchen floor. I am confronted with a choice: Which should I do first? Wipe the muddy paws before he decorates the entire floor or clean up the semi-digested mess? Both tasks are admittedly short term but neither is appealing and I have to choose which to do first. Please note the role of values: my values assume that both cleaning tasks have to be done. Experience tells me that my husband will not be doing either task because 1) he would probably add to one mess, and 2) he would say that the dog's paws are not really all that dirty. See… experience, values, and decisions play a part in a simple behavior over which I might not feel as though I have a choice, yet I do. I select my choice based on my experiences and values. FYI – dirty paws first. Oh, I could talk/encourage a different behavior from my husband, but it is not that important to me. Values again.

We apply our values sometimes consciously and sometimes instinctively. Some of our values are constant throughout our lives and some shift given our experiences, age, education, and health. We typically make choices that are most consistent with furthering our values, however limited we may say or feel our choices are.

If our decisions are in line with our values, we feel stronger and happier than if we make a decision that is contrary to our values. In that case we are unhappy and spend considerable energy complaining about our plight and trying to make ourselves feel better.

The driving force for many of the 123 mothers in my longitudinal study was a personal, deep-seated value, but the value was very different for employed mothers than that of at-home mothers.

According to the responses and behaviors, employed mothers wrote about achievement and independence:

> I need to have a sense of career accomplishment beyond motherhood.
> I have always been a hardworking, competent person.
> I have also been very independent.

The at-home mothers' comments focused on nurturing and caring:

> Once my children were born, I knew in my soul that I had to be home with them.
>
> I wanted to be available for my kids whenever circumstances required it.

The mothers had different values and different priorities about what was most important to them. At a given time and given their personal situations, the mothers chose the work status that was in line with what they valued most.

Another factor that influences how we feel is our need for support and confirmation that we are good mothers and wives, and interesting, competent adults. Each of us reaches out and receives this information in different ways. In general, employed mothers usually bond with other employed mothers. They offer support with the challenges and stresses they feel from trying to balance the demands of home and employment. They also seek and share practical advice about where or how to manage logistics, tantrums, food allergies. Employed mothers get confirmation that they are good mothers from other employed mothers. They also receive feedback about themselves as thinking, intelligent women through performance evaluations and promotions. A great deal of their feelings of competence stem from the evaluations and measures of success they receive from their employment experiences and superiors.

Stay-at-home mothers also need validation as good mothers and as adult women. If they are not getting these rewards from parenting, volunteer, or social activities, they often feel they are "missing something" by not being in the workforce. However, if they feel rewarded for their efforts in these areas, they will be happy and have plenty of energy to fulfill their responsibilities to their family, themselves, and others in the community.

Often when people ask an at-home mother what she does all day, she chooses answers that demonstrate achievement such as: "Doing our finances, planning vacations, overseeing contractors, or volunteering at the church or library." What some mothers carefully do not say is that they spend time talking with girlfriends. Sitting around talking with girlfriends and eating bon-bons is what people think if they assume an at-home mother does not really do anything with her time. The truth is, when a mother is talking with girlfriends, she is taking care of herself. When she talks about her children, her husband, and whatever else is on her mind she is seeking confirmation or support about how she is handling situations, the people involved and what she is thinking—even intellectual thoughts! In short, she gets affirmation that she is a good mother and a good wife that may well include support on how to better handle an issue or person; she is not alone and she is understood. All during these conversations, she is generally receiving good feelings about herself as a woman, adult, and thinking person.

Unlike her counterpart, the employed mother who within the work environment finds others like herself, the at-home mother has to be resourceful—she has to locate other at-home mothers if they do not live next door:

As I've mentioned above, the circumstances intertwined with values often change over time. This includes what a mother-to-be might think about her work status once she has a family. If we are aware of how our values—our feelings— play out in different situations, we might handle the new situations with more confidence.

Some of us may discuss with our husbands how life will be when we start a family. It is a serious discussion and each of us tries to be honest to the best of our ability. What neither knows for certain is how we will feel and what the reality of the situation will be when, in fact, we become a family. None of us, not one of us, can be certain how we will feel about a situation until we are actually experiencing it.

For instance, if a woman who has been practicing in a large, competitive law firm becomes pregnant with her first child, she may then ask herself the following series of questions:

1) Do I/Can I stay in this firm, work 60 to 80 hours a week to become partner and still take care of my baby/family?

2) Do I/Can I find a job in the government or with an association or company where the hours most probably will be more reasonable but I may not get the "career success" or money that I anticipated/wanted?

3) Do I/Can I find a position in a small firm that practices real estate law or financial planning that will not require the lengthy and odd hours and will provide an opportunity for partnership but at a lower financial or maybe "prestigious level"?

4) Do I/Can I try to practice on my own and work at-home?

Mother-to-be raises the above questions on the assumption that her husband will be supportive of her employment and the added responsibility and time it takes to raise a family. Although 88 percent of the mothers in my study confirmed that their spouses were supportive of their work status, a reading of their comments that followed revealed a different story. About a third of the employed mothers wrote comments claiming either their husbands wanted them more at home, or they did not provide as much support to family activities as was needed or desired by the employed mothers

The following comments by mothers in my study about the support they received from their husbands are followed by a generalization of the issue suggested by the comment and then related value questions. Each gives an idea of how every situation evokes a discussion of values and subsequent choices that can affect work status decisions.

>Comment: "Even though I had the more demanding job and hours, somehow whenever a child was sick, I was the one that stayed home."

>Issue: Who stays home if the baby is sick? Or there is any health problem or a more long-term health problem?

>Value: Do you always need or want to be the one who cares for an ill child?

>Comment: "He was wonderful, did all the food shopping and even cooked dinner. I'm so lucky."
>
>>OR
>
>"I could always count on him to pick up the children and take them to soccer practice."

Issue: Who will take care of the tasks (clean house, make dinner, food shop, fix appliances, etc.) necessary to run a household?

OR

Who will take care of the tasks/logistics of making sure that your children meet commitments and remain engaged in society?

Value: Is taking care of the logistics enough? What about the cognitive, physical, psychological, and social growth of each child?

Comment: "He was always there for me, whatever I wanted as long as I was happy."

Issue: Who cares for the relationships between and among family members?

Value: How important is communication about feelings and expectations? Could you leave this to your husband, do it yourself, or must it be a partnership?

The above scenarios regarding spousal support provide examples of how daily communication and behaviors involve circumstances, values, and choices that can affect our work status decisions and our sense of selves. We cannot predict the circumstances, but we can become more aware that each event and each decision is a choice filled with values that do impact our family and our self-esteem, even though they may seem isolated or insignificant at the time. Not every decision is life changing. However, being cognizant may help us navigate these ever-changing waters concerning our family and ourselves.

The financial, health, education, employment circumstances that you, your children, your parents have will change over time. Your values—what you identify as important to you and your family that affect how you evaluate situations—also may change over time. Whenever a major change occurs that impacts the family or any individual member – particularly you and your spouse—it would be a good idea to chat again. What you want is for each of you—and you are important—to feel good about yourself as a parent, a spouse, and an adult. Life will not be a panacea; it is hard raising a family. It is challenging to take care of a home, all domestic tasks as well as the physical, intellectual, emotional, and psychological development of each family member, the family as a unit, and no less important, the marriage. If we pay attention to our ever-changing circumstances and values and acknowledge our choices, we may feel more empowered to make decisions that are best for us and our family.

Chapter 2

What Do I Tell My Daughters*?

"What do I tell my daughters?" was what one mother wanted to know after she received some statistical results from my study. She thought they were "nice," but not what she really wanted to know. What she really wanted to know was "what do I tell my daughters? Do I tell them to stay at home or remain employed when they become mothers?"

My first reaction to her question was OMG, what a good question! I wonder what I have told my own daughter (and son) about employment after becoming a parent. Here I was conducting a study on mothers' decisions regarding work status and I was not sure what my own children thought—great mom. So... I first emailed my daughter and asked her what overt or covert message I gave her about working outside the home once/if (I have to be careful about assumptions) she becomes a mother. She immediately phoned me asking "Is everything ok?" Startled, I asked why and she said," You sounded so serious..." I explained the reason for my email. "Oh, that's easy," she said. "The clear message was that it's very important for the parents to be there for their children. That's not to say one can't have a career, but I guess if possible, a parent should be home with the children at least for the first several years."

---

* The term "daughters" is used in this chapter solely because this is the specific question a mother in the study asked. All that is said can definitely apply to "sons" too.

Believing in equality of the sexes, I then phoned my son. "I was wondering if you were going to ask me," he ventured. Clearly pleased to be asked he said, "That's interesting because we [he and his fiancée] were discussing this very question. We decided that ideally one of us, whether for three or six months or a year, would be home with the children and then we'd switch off. This of course would be ideal; we have no idea what reality will be."[†]

Although I frequently talked with my children and probably gave more "lectures" on how one "should" handle a situation or behave, than they wanted to hear, I do not think I ever actually discussed my thoughts regarding their future choices about being an at-home parent or pursuing employment. Consequently, their responses must have been based on their reactions to their observations about our family life; in this instance, my work status decisions, which were simple. I went from an at-home mother involved in school and community activities and my dissertation to part-time employment—teaching a college course, when they were in secondary school. I was at home until they left for school and returned home well before they finished their school day.

The mother mentioned above however, told her daughters (16 and 20 years old) never to quit working. She had to stop her career because her husband traveled a lot and her children needed her at home. Now, however, she is working and is very happy.

Can we tell our children what to do? We all know that answer—"no." Well, we can tell them what we think they might

---

[†] They are now married, have a child, and my son is an assistant professor. His wife is finishing her dissertation and looking for a post-doctoral position or employment. Their baby—my grandson—is in day care. See? We have opinions but do not know what we are going to do until the time comes.

consider but whether or not they choose to follow our words of wisdom is something different. First, they observe our behavior—what we do and how we feel about our choices. We have no control over how they interpret what they observe.

What we can say is that finding their own answer about employment or staying home is not simple and it is not the same for everyone. Each of the mothers in the study made decisions about their work status based on their values, experiences, and current situation. Even their decisions were not a constant; they sometimes changed their work status as their current situation changed, or their experience changed which in turn might have changed their values.

What we may be able to do is help our children think through what is embodied in the question: Employment or stay at-home? Before saying a word, it might be best to ask ourselves what we know about our children's values, circumstances, and experiences. Starting with values, do our daughters have our same values? Well, we all hope that our children incorporate some of our values. Experience tells us, though, that our children may have some, maybe most of our values, but not all of our values. Not a point of discussion. If we want to continue open communication with our children, we best accept that some of their values may not match our own; they are not us. They are people in their own right with different experiences, perceptions and, yes, probably different values.

Now, what about your daughter's current situation? If this is a "I'm just thinking about..." but not married or no children yet, then the truth is, this is a big hypothetical discussion and just listen and agree if you want future chats on this subject. The reasoning behind this is that we never know for sure what we are going to do in a situation until we are actually in the situation.

Frequently, studies use freshman psychology students as the research populations. Students tend to think they know what they will do based on what they think they want now. Yet, what they think and how they will actually behave when in a particular situation is often not the same. This is not to put down freshmen psychology students; this is human nature. We never know for sure how we will act or feel until we are in the situation. Unless your daughter is a mother, the situation is not real and the discussion is thus, hypothetical.

As one mother observed:

I started to see from experience that women couldn't accurately predict whether they would return to work or stay home before the first child arrived. It was a decision made after the child arrived.

It remains hypothetical even if she is pregnant. Once she has the baby, then the situation becomes real. What if the baby has medical problems...? (We all hope not, but...) What if the baby is cranky or a very quiet introverted child, the opposite of the mother's outgoing personality? How will the mother respond? How will she feel? Maybe she will instinctively love the challenge of calming an unsettled infant. Maybe she will love patiently nurturing a shy child. But what if she does not? What if it is very hard and frustrating for her? What if she gets more satisfaction from her career? More kudos? What if the mother is happiest when reassured about herself as a person—a capable, good person—based on external evaluations found regularly in the workplace? Maybe she and her baby would do better if she spent shorter spells with the infant and did so when she felt good about herself as a competent person.

These are dynamics concerning the interaction between two personalities that we do not know about until we experience them. How the interaction makes us feel is an important experience that strongly affects decision making, leading to a decision that is personal and right for that one individual. Not a decision for an outsider to make, or on which to pass judgment.

What other elements might we assess that comprise our situation; in this instance, the situations of our children? These include: the strength and communication of the marriage; the finances of family now and future expectations; education, employment, and career opportunities; health of all members of the family; and living style choices, among others. It is worth noting that we only know what we are told or perceive about a situation; we do not know or understand completely what others know and feel. In short, we know our children, but not everything about them and not everything about their situations as well as relationships with others.

A simple example is that no one knows what really goes on in a marriage besides the married couple. All the rest of us only know what we observe and are told. Further complicating our understanding on this subject is that our observations are not fact; they are our perceptions that, of course, are colored by our own experiences, situations, and values.

What relationship is not fraught with perceptions and misperceptions rather than facts? People bring to a relationship their perception and interpretation of what the other is doing. Without intention, one person can hurt the feelings of another—a case of a misperception or misinterpretation of a behavior. A particular relationship often filled with misperceptions is the tried and true mother-daughter relationship. The mothers in this study who said they chose the opposite work status from that of their mothers did so because they felt ignored. Given the assumption that all mothers do the very best they can and do love their children, I doubt the mothers meant for their children to feel ignored.

Several mothers in the study said that they decided to stay home with their children because their mothers were employed and they resented their absence. These mothers wanted to be more available to their children. Some of their comments below exemplify this sentiment:

> When I was 12, my mom went back to work and I felt abandoned. I was also given lots of responsibility that I resented. I didn't want to do that to my kids.

> She was home physically, but she was always working, she never went to my back to school nights or was involved in my schools. She worked late into the night. I resented it and felt (not altogether unfairly) that her work was more important to her than we were. It was very important to me that I not do that to my children. I wanted them to know they were the most important thing to me (besides my husband) in

the world and they still are. Is there any job more important than that?

I loved having my mom home.... I felt impoverished when my parents bought a store for my mom to run. ...it seemed like I hardly ever saw her. Our home was never the same again.

And of course, people being different, there were mothers in the study whose choice about their work status was influenced by wanting to do what their mothers did:

I believe my parents have always been my role models .... They were both well-educated with interesting careers and outside interests. ... I hope my husband I and have such a positive influence on our own children.

My mother...encouraged me to continue working full time because she believed that was how I would be happiest. She continued to inform me that my daughters would be just fine.

The above quotes were in reaction to their mothers' employment when they were children. The first group resented the absence of their mother in the home and wanted to provide a different experience for their children. The second group emulated their mothers' employment outside of the home. What about reactions to mothers who were at home when they were children?

> Two mothers in the study claimed that they were inspired to do as their mothers did and stay at home with their children:
> I wanted to parent my children the way my parents raised me except I would eliminate some of the negative stuff and accentuate the positive.
>
> My mom...stayed at home with us. ...I really wanted my kids to have the same warm home experience that I had had.

To round off the above comments of mothers doing the same or the opposite as their employed mothers and some doing the same as their at-home mothers, I searched for mothers in the study who wrote that their mothers had stayed at home and they were "not going to do that!" There were not any quotes. Why? Is it because by 1994 having a career or employment instead of being at home with the children was an accepted choice and mothers no longer had to "fight" to participate in the workforce? They assumed that their mothers had no choice and now they do?

As I mentioned in the introduction, back in 1963, Betty Friedan, author of *The Feminine Mystique*, challenged the pervasive social idea that a woman's place was in the home and that it was a personal fulfilling role. I had the opportunity to actually talk briefly with Ms. Friedan in the late '90s and had a rather amusing conversation with her, which supports the notion that staying at home was not necessarily the expected or perhaps even desired choice of mothers by then.

I was at an American Association of University Women luncheon and Ms. Friedan was the guest speaker. My friend was the president of the local chapter so when the guest of honor arrived and was sitting by herself, my friend came over to where a few of us were standing pleading for someone to go talk to her.

Not being shy, and interested in meeting her, I marched myself over to where she was seated. Ms. Friedan had no interest in making polite conversation. So I asked her what she thought of my being an at-home mother. She gruffly asked, "What?!" I repeated my question to the same response not once, but twice! She then dismissingly said, "Oh, I thought you said you were an asshole mother!" I responded that I was not, that actually I thought I was a rather good mother, but what did she think of one being at-home? She clearly wasn't very inspired to pursue this line of questioning but answered that maybe I would eventually seek employment. Perhaps Ms. Friedan fought so hard for women to be able to seek employment and career fulfillment outside of the home that she was unable to imagine that a woman would knowingly want to stay at home with her children.

In addition to the mother-daughter relationship that influences a mother's work status is her relationship with her husband. A young woman related her brother's phone calls complaining about his wife who was never home. His wife was a resident in obstetrics and was at the hospital for long hours and often called to work in the middle of the night or on weekends. He, who worked at home, was very frustrated that she wasn't home more to help care for their two young children.

His sister said to him, "Do not complain to me! Where were you when she was applying to medical school? Did you think she was doing that for fun and then would quit and stay home with the children? Where were you when she was deciding to focus on obstetrics? Were you unaware of the time and commitment required by doctors in obstetrics?"

The bottom line of this very wise sister's remarks is: before you marry him, listen to his dreams and what he wants to do. And, more importantly for you, pay attention to how he listens to your dreams and what you want to do. If he's not listening and valuing what you want, the chances of his being supportive to your career efforts are limited.

One of the questions I asked the mothers was "How did your spouse demonstrate his support of your work status?" The highest percentage (55%) was of at-home mothers who thought their husbands were okay with their stay-at-home work status. Thirty-seven percent of the employed mothers felt a lack of spousal support because 1) they were either divorced, or 2) their husbands were "not thrilled with my working full time," or 3) "being a little selfish." (*See* Appendix, Graph 1.)

One mother wrote:

> He was delighted and encouraged my working full time because he liked the money I earned. Of course, I also continued to be completely responsible for the children and the house!

As mothers, all we can do to guide our children is be aware that we are role models—our children are observing our behavior. We can also share with them our frustrations or challenges and, more important, how we change or handle these issues. We cannot tell them what to do. And, as we heard from the earlier comments about following their mothers' work status, they do not necessarily, do as we do either.

So... what do we tell them? We tell them to think about what their current circumstances are—financial, educational, employment, health of all family members—and what their values are. We encourage our daughters to make decisions about their work status based on what is best for them and their family and, as much as possible, have these decisions consistent with their values. We tell them that if a decision is contrary to their values they may well feel frustrated and unhappy, which leads to a waste of energy because they will spend a lot of time trying to feel better about themselves and the life they have currently carved out for themselves and their family.

The 123 mothers in my study changed their decisions about employment many times. Each time, circumstances or experiences had changed which altered their priorities regarding themselves and their families. As long as their decisions were in line with their values, they were happy, had energy for their "work" whether a career or as an at-home mother, and felt good about themselves. What more do we want for our children?

Chapter 3

Is There An Ideal Work Status?

Unfortunately, there is no Holy Grail work status for all mothers. Given that each mother identifies situations relevant to her work status and then applies her personal values, it is no wonder there is no "agreement" about any one work status being "the answer" for all mothers. Each mother has her own circumstances and values, so no work status would or could be right for all. However, there is good news. Mothers, who at any time experienced full-time, part-time employment, or being at-home full time, enumerated very satisfying aspects in each of the work status options. Of course, they also identified frustrating parts of each work status option.

Full-time employment

Taking the responses of all the mothers in the study, 57 percent of those who were, at any time, employed full time wrote that there just was not enough time to respond to the demands of the job, their children, household, and their own needs. All these demands created a lot of stress, which they found very frustrating:

> Not enough time to balance work and family. I feel like I am not totally organized—always trying to catch up on things.

> The stress of having to make it home through terrible traffic in time to relieve the daycare/afterschool care provider.

> Trying to fulfill my boss's expectations and my own desires to get ahead, with the demands for my time and attention from my children and husband.

The responses above clearly describe the challenges of being pulled in one direction to be the best employee and in another direction to be the best mother and wife you can be. Just dealing with the objective factors of time, place, and the accompanying responsibilities can be very taxing.

Trying to be excellent in two roles can and does lead to more subjective issues that were also identified as frustrating, but this time by 35 percent of the mothers. These factors include exhaustion, stress, and no time to think about, never mind care for, yourself.

A mother who was employed full time and traveled frequently, who retired to be an at-home mother when her children were in high school stated:

> I always felt rushed, stressed and exhausted because there were many demands from work and at the home front. Had a hard time relaxing and sleeping through the night. Also, wished I didn't have to miss some of my children's special activities.

> Long hours, stress, inability to give my family all that was needed, no down time for myself, constant demands on my time and energy, feeling burned out.

An interesting observation from a full-time employed mother suggests the self-imposed "mommy track" she chose to reduce her stress. This evidently came with the small price of guilt:

> The main reward for working hard in the government is that you receive more work and responsibility, which ultimately creates more role strain for a mother. The alternative, not working very hard, actually worked better for mothers, it seemed to me, but I always felt guilty not working hard since I was working for the taxpayers (federal employee).

Given these quotes of frustration and stress, it is no wonder that there are books written to help mothers handle the logistics of two roles/two jobs.

Juggling: The Unexpected Advantage of Balancing Career and Home for Women and Their Families, (Crosby, 1991) was one of the first books published advising employed mothers how to handle both roles with a sense of humor. "The unexpected advantage" part espouses that the children and husbands of employed mothers were happier. I am not going to discuss that in detail. But, let me just say it is the kind of comment that is more self-serving than fact.

Another book, *Mothers on the Fast Track: How a Generation Can Balance Family and Careers,* (Mason and Mason Ekman, 2007), although focused on how to climb the corporate ladder and not remain in lower levels of management because of the demands of motherhood, does provide suggestions for creating an optimum balance between work and home.

Advice is out there to help full-time employed mothers find a balance between the demands of employment and motherhood. And note that within the advice is critical information that will confirm you are not alone. The information will validate your daily efforts often filled with stress. We all feel better about ourselves when we realize there are others out there who are like us with similar struggles, successes and failures; they understand.

I was on a panel recently at a conference sponsored by Congressman Jim Moran on "Living My Ideal Life: Balancing Career, Family and Personal Needs." During the Q and A a young mother who had brought her very energetic three year old with her because she had no one or could not afford to pay someone to watch her child, asked for help on how to manage as a single mother. She was going to school to better her job options and make more money to support herself and her son. She did not have enough time in the day, enough money to manage everything, or enough help; she was exhausted and felt alone.

All mothers in the session—no dads, except my husband who came to support me—started to offer suggestions. What really seemed to make a difference to her were the comments that included: "I know, I've been there," and "You're doing a wonderful job managing everything" and "Yes, it is very hard but you seem to be handling it!" We all like confirmation that we are doing a good job and respected for our efforts; our struggles, though unique to us, are typical. We need the support of knowing that we can and we actually are meeting the challenges.

If full-time employment is filled with stress and frustration, what is so satisfying that counters these uncomfortable feelings? We are not masochists; we do not choose to remain in situations that we find unpleasant, so what is the pull to keep so many employed full time? The answer is: the tangible rewards we receive from employment—promotions, power, money—plus the personal growth and achievements we experience. In fact, a total of 89 percent of the mothers in the study who experienced full-time employment at any time cited either the tangible "rewards of the job" (51%) or the "personal growth and accomplishments" (38%) as very satisfying.

The quotes below exemplify the satisfaction the mothers gained from full-time employment. You can almost hear their pride:

> Respect, appreciation, socializing with co-workers, prestige, independence, money for extras.

> A sense of accomplishment at work—especially when I was able to get a big project finished that really made a difference. Getting to the point where I had extensive knowledge of the organization and how to make things happen.

> To be perfectly honest, it isn't the work that is particularly satisfying—it is the fact that I have excellent benefits with the federal government—health benefits, pension plan, thrift savings, etc.

> The reward of being able to do things for my family that I could not have done without the income I earned... If I had not worked I do not know that we could have had as many great travel experiences. Also—I am the "toy" buyer: iPods, computer stuff...all from mom's salary!

These quotes from different mothers in my study are filled with a sense of pride and solid self-esteem. The mothers clearly gained a strong sense of competence about themselves and their abilities, which they value very much. Whether you gain a sense of competence from money, promotions, achievements, or all three, they certainly do boost your self-esteem. Full-time employment provides the opportunities to obtain these feelings.

Further confirmation that full-time employment has very satisfying rewards is that a total of 91 percent of the full-time employed mothers found "rewards—promotions, raises, and salary—of the job (49%)" or "personal growth and accomplishments (42%)" very satisfying. Given that 80 percent of the mothers who were employed full time in 1994 remained in full-time employment in 2008, it is safe to surmise that these tangible rewards and the personal rewards obtained in full-time employment outweigh the frustration and stress experienced by most of these mothers. (*See* Appendix, Graph 2.)

Another interesting finding is that in 2008 more part-time employed mothers than any other work status group—71 percent—wrote that "rewards of the job" was very satisfying. What makes this interesting is that 37 percent of these mothers were at home in 1994 compared to the 15 percent who were employed full time in 1994—more than double.

Why is that? Why did the mothers who were at home for any length of time really value and appreciate the rewards of employment (part-time employment 71%) more than those who were employed full time (49%)? If we think about the kind of satisfaction a mother at home receives compared to a full-time employed mother, we'll get an answer.

The compensations a mother at home receives are personal and emotional—often self-observed; they are not clear, tangible, objective rewards. At-home mothers do not have performance reviews. They do not receive a salary. They do not get promoted; a promotion isn't even possible! And, in truth, not very often do mothers at home hear: "You're doing a great job;" "You handled the kids' argument well;" or even, "Thank you for making a delicious dinner." Or, "The way you managed getting a baby sitter for the kids and planned our vacation was superb—so organized, fun, and easy." I could go on and on….but need I say more?

You get the picture. Full-time employment offers ongoing assessments and if you are a good employee, you receive lots of kudos in different ways that tell you are good, smart, and competent. As one mother commented in 1994:

> One of the biggest challenges I faced when I stopped [working] seven years ago was being able to derive satisfaction from staying home. I missed the pay raises, promotions, and praise from superiors. Now that our children are seven and three, I am able to

derive a lot of satisfaction from my "role" in raising my children. Their happiness, independence, self-confidence, good manners, and compassion towards others are my feedback.

Understandably, it is hard to give up the rewards of successful employment. This is probably a good thing, otherwise the stresses and frustrations would prevail and no one would choose full-time employment.

What about part-time employment, the work status often touted as the ideal? While it is not ideal—no work status is—many (62%) of the mothers who ever worked part time found it a good balance between employment and family. And more than the other two work status groups, the mothers who were employed full time in 2008 cited part-time employment as providing a "good balance." (*See* Appendix, Graph 3.)

Given that most of these full-time employed mothers were frustrated by trying to address the needs of both family and employer, it is no wonder they definitely valued the extra hours they had when they experience part-time employment. The extra hours enabled them to give more time to their families.

To give words to these results, below are some comments on the balance of part-time employment from mothers employed full time in 2008:

At work, recognition for a job well done...being present for my children's especially fun or meaningful activities.

> More time with children, less stress, more flexibility.

> I love, love, love the freedom to exercise and take care of errands for children.

As I have mentioned, we are not all the same. We have different experiences, circumstances, and values. Thus, some of us would not find part-time employment a "good balance." And, in fact, the mothers found definite reasons to find part-time employment frustrating. More than half of the mothers who were ever employed part time—like those who were ever employed full time—cited logistics and time as frustrating about part-time employment. Further, another 26 percent were aggravated by the expectations of others and having too much to do:

> Everyone wants to give you things to do with your "spare time." As a volunteer for a professional association, I was indirectly asked to take phone reservations from members for the upcoming luncheon ("since you have so much free time"); as a parent, I was asked to become room mother; as a worker, I was asked to come in on my days off. I had to learn to smile and say "no." The reason I wanted to work part time was to have more time with my children and to choose the activities that I wanted to do to bring balance to my life.

> Not enough salary for the hours of work involved, increased expectations from my family that I can do all the errands and chores because I'm not really working any more.
>
> Always having more to do ... everywhere, at home and at work.
>
> I didn't feel that I was a success at either the mothering or the work because I was doing both at once.

One mother who learned from past experience that remuneration from part-time employment was skimpy compared to that of full-time employment—no benefits and less pay—were adding to her frustrations:

> Part-time was never part time. After going on part time status once in the early 1990's, I realized "part-time" was part time pay for full time work. The second time I did it, I negotiated an hourly rate because I knew 25 hours/week would usually turn into 60 hours/week, and I was right.
>
> Limitations on career mobility.
>
> No benefits. Inability to schedule totally around the children—if you're giving up money for flexibility,

then it should be as flexible as you want. If not, you might as well work full time.

Is part-time employment a better option than full-time employment? Both have the frustration of being pulled in two directions—caring for family versus excelling at employment. And, although both employment groups—full and part time, cite personal growth and accomplishments as rewards of employment, their primary source of satisfaction is different.

Most of the mothers in the study cited the tangible rewards, e.g., promotions, money, power, prestige, to be particularly satisfying about full-time employment. However, for part-time employment, the mothers most frequently named a good balance as the most satisfying quality, the same aspect they found frustrating about part-time employment. Why would this be? Was there one work status group that more frequently cited the "good balance" as satisfying?

If we look closer at the responses and examine what percent of each work status group actually wrote that a "good balance" was the most satisfying aspect of part-time employment, it turns out that the full-time employed mothers represented 51 percent of the mothers in that category compared to 26 and 23 percent of the part-time employed and at-home mothers in 2008. That makes sense because part-time employment is seen as lessening the tug-of-war between home and office and giving more time to mothers to attend to their children, which is the big cause of frustration from full-time employment.

You, your circumstances, your values, and your experiences will determine if part-time employment is a better employment option for you than full-time employment. As you can conclude from the mothers in my study, both have their frustrations and benefits.

Full-Time at Home

These frustrations and concerns about employment lead us to the final option:
what about staying at home and taking care of your family, spouse, and home? Is this a panacea? What is the effect of putting aside your career aspirations to raise your children? What about following your passion to be at home for your children?

Like full- and part-time employment, being at home has its frustration—frustrations that are unique to that work status. Looking at all the responses from the mothers in my study, almost 75% of them claimed that the most frustrating aspects of being an at-home mother were the isolation they felt and the lack of structure in their lives. Below are some quotes expressing these frustrations:

> This is the first job I've had without a "performance description"—sometimes it's very hard to know if I'm on the mark. Sometimes it is easier to perform to someone else's standards.

> Being isolated. Feeling that nothing was being accomplished.

The lack of sleep and adult conversation. I think when things are crazy at home you feel frustrated that you are "wasting" your education and skills dealing with mundane matters.

Boredom, loneliness and frustration.

If you have these feelings of loneliness and isolation, all very common and understandable, ask yourself, "Is there something I can possibly do about the situation?"

To do something about these circumstances requires a certain amount of personal resourcefulness, which I think, based on the responses throughout both of my studies, is an important quality to exercise if you decide to be a stay-at-home mother. By proactively seeking and finding activities, friends, people, and even perhaps, other mothers, you can make sure you are not alone and have adult contact. However, remember, these opportunities will not just magically appear. You have to find them. This will, unfortunately, not provide a salary or professional status, but it will provide adult conversation and lessen the feeling of being alone. There are also other benefits from seeking out others. You can share concerns, interests, and be validated for what you are doing, how you are feeling about all your roles—mother, wife, woman, adult, even daughter or daughter-in-law.

I realize I am saying this as an extrovert—I like and am comfortable being around people; I often prefer being or talking with other people to being by myself. If you are an introvert, then you probably often feel more comfortable being alone. However, being alone can/may lead to loneliness, particularly, if you are in a new place in life. If you find others—some may even be introverts like you—you may discover that you are not alone; others have similar feelings and what you are experiencing is okay, even good.

We all need validation for who we are; we can give that to ourselves. But at some point, we may need it from others. It is up to us to go find others or maybe circumstances that reinforce who we are and give us confidence to continue or make adjustments. The journey can be shared and does not need to be done solo; you are not alone and need not feel alone.

Do keep in mind that employed mothers seek each other out to give support for their struggles as employed mothers. A friend of mine, who always had full-time employment, said, "I never could have made it without my friend and co-worker. She was a constant source of support and provided great ideas for any concerns I had from the time our children were babies to even now— and they are grown up." All mothers need support for their choices and actions; it is up to you to make sure you get it for yourself. You deserve it.

Another mother articulates that accomplishments are few and far between:

> Having a four year old and a newborn baby, seven days a week… Having all day and "nothing" to show for it. One day when I was feeling I hadn't accomplished a thing, I wrote down what I did that day. I was amazed at what I was calling "nothing."

I would love to know what was on her list because I do not remember what I did all day. When you are home with a baby, little gets accomplished and you can often spend a lot of time alone, "accomplishing nothing." Being at home with babies and toddlers is very demanding of your time. I can remember some mornings thinking "right after I change and feed the baby I will take a shower." Do not ask me what I was doing or where the time went, but when I next looked at the clock it was 2:00 and I had not yet made it to the shower!

I know that somehow most babies are fed, bathed, dressed in relatively clean clothes, played with, exposed to other people and places, and manage to grow up. All of these activities are accomplishments and certainly critical to a baby's well-being. We would best not call our daily activities "nothing"; rather, if we could, choose to take satisfaction in what we do get done.

Two truly excellent books—both by Ann Crittenden—denounce this concept that at-home mothers "do and accomplish nothing." Crittenden's first book, *The Price of Motherhood: Why the Most Important Job in the World Is Still the Least Valued* (Metropolitan Books/2001), discusses how our social practices do not value the work of mothers. And her second, *If You've Raised Kids You Can Manage Anything* (October 2005), demonstrates how as mothers we learn and perform many skills that are similar to managers in the workplace: multitasking, negotiating, motivating techniques. Both are very interesting reads.

Another source of frustration experienced by at-home mothers is the loss of a sense of self. If you stay home, if you leave your employment, then you are no longer a lawyer, secretary, manager, sales woman or whatever occupation "defined" you. You, according to society, are suddenly nobody.

Do not believe it. You are many things. You are an at-home mother growing your children to be the best people they can be—people who are good citizens, good employees and employers; good, kind, thoughtful people who may become spouses and parents. Still, you have no title that many people in the employment world consider of value. In addition to that, you have no money of your own unless you are very lucky and 1) inherited it or 2) worked very hard and saved a lot—that is not most of us.

Some examples of this loss are cited below:

> I felt like I lost a part of myself—my focus was totally on my children. I became more dependent on my husband and deferred to him to make decisions that I would have made myself prior to having children.

> Felt I was disappearing.

> My feelings are that stay-at-home moms are underrated and underappreciated.

I know this feeling. Occasionally, I would become really annoyed with my family for their seeming assumption that I would just "do" for them. They expressed no appreciation that I could see. I got really tired of being taken for granted. So, every once in a while I would yell at all of them telling them that "I was tired of being taken for granted and they could do everything (usually dinner) for themselves." Silence... and surprise. And then I got the appreciation for a while until... many months later, the scene repeated itself—maybe three times in all. I felt better and they needed shaping up.

Not having your own money can also be very difficult and hard on your sense of self as an adult. You become financially dependent on your husband. Many marriages handle this situation well so that neither spouse feels used or helpless concerning the finances. Other times, as some of you may have experienced, being dependent on your spouse can cause problems. It can be hard on your sense of self as an independent adult not to be able to buy what you think you or your family or the house needs, or to buy a surprise gift for your husband without his knowledge or asking his "permission." Sometimes, a little surprise gift for yourself is nice too!

The frustration and possible subsequent problem of not having your own income is expressed here:

> Totally financially dependent on my husband who was resentful.

> Not having some discretionary income (to buy gifts for my husband, for one thing).

Finances are funny. Each person has his or her own feelings and treatment about money. How money was handled and thought about in your family when you were a child plays a big part in how you think about money as an adult. Your spouse...same dynamics. It is hard to change those ideas and those feelings.

A friend of mine and her husband both work full time. She said that they share all financial responsibilities easily and evenly. If one of them needs money to pay a bill, they just ask—neither cares or keeps track. However, because she comes from a background in which she really prides herself on her earnings, she knows she can sometimes be extra sensitive to "handing over" some of her cash. She became really annoyed when they needed money to pay for a large and unexpected bill that came to her husband even though she rationally knew all such bills really belonged to both of them. She had just received a bonus at work equal to the amount needed. He happily suggested they use her bonus to pay the bill. She was incensed: "But that is MY bonus!" Letting go can be difficult; sometimes your initial reactions, your gut feelings, aren't always rational. These attitudes are sensitive and hard to change. I think the best we can do is honestly examine our attitudes and discuss them. (I believe that because they communicated well about their respective sensitivities, she kept her bonus and they found the money elsewhere.)

Although problematic financial issues, the frustrations of loneliness, and loss of sense of self are important and worth noting, if you are thinking of being an at-home mother, there are also wonderful satisfactions. The mothers in my study identified three types of rewards they received from being home caring for their children: 1) being there for my children, watching and helping with their development (49%); 2) the personal freedom I had to do activities with the kids, volunteer in the community and at school, plus a little time for myself (39%); and 3) creating a welcoming home and/or fulfilling God's wishes (14%).

My original—1994—study, at-home mothers definitely had different sources of satisfaction from the employed mothers. Approximately 57 percent of the mothers who were at home in 1994 found satisfaction from being able to be there for their children and watching and helping with their development, whereas 78 percent of the employed mothers valued "personal freedom and time for community and to be with kids." (*See* Appendix, Graph 4.) The satisfaction at-home mothers felt about watching their children grow does not directly counter the frustration of loneliness and definitely not the lack of adult communication, but it does address the passion to nurture and be with their children and the general lack of stress from having to balance the demands of employment and home.

As some mothers said in my 1994 study:

All in all I've tried working when I had kids and I was miserable. I could not leave my kids with anyone else—I just couldn't.

I liked knowing about my kids' experiences and how different experiences affected them. I was with them so I was aware of many aspects of their lives. This helped me be more in touch with them. I knew what made them happy and, if they were having a bad day, I knew why. I didn't need to have them ask for help or support. I could read them so well I was able to offer it before they even knew they needed it sometimes.

I'll never have regrets that I missed my kids' childhood, the privilege of being the person they count on, seeing them grow independent, seeing that they appreciate what I've given them.

Having time for self and the freedom to do activities with the children and work in the community was another category created by 27 percent of mothers who were at home in 1994. This same "freedom" category was cited by 78 percent of the mothers who were employed full time in 1994 but were at some time over the 14 years at home with their children. This personal freedom to spend time with their kids, volunteer in the community, and have time for themselves was critical to their satisfaction of being at home with their children.

The responses of the full-time employed mothers are consistent with, and an extension of, their satisfaction with part-time employment. They are trying to balance employment with caring for their family. Being at home full time removed the tension or pull from employment. All energy and time could be devoted to the family, the community, and even leave some time for herself.

Below are a few quotes from full-time employed mothers about their appreciation for the personal freedom experienced when they were at home full time:

> Family functioned better, had dinner together every night, everyone loved having great food, never felt stressed (since I knew what real stress was, I didn't let little things at home stress me out), got to finally do my share of volunteer work.

Not feeling pulled in another direction and having time and learning new hobbies, e.g., painting.

Stress-free; get back into fitness routine; get better connected with myself physically and mentally; take yoga and meditation classes; make new friends.

These employed mothers appreciated the "free" time—no demands from employment—they experienced when they were at home full time.

Do not forget, most of these mothers (80%) did not remain at home. The pleasure of focused time allotted by no employment did not override their passions, their pride from the rewards of employment, and their gains in self-esteem. These feelings of satisfaction kept them in the workforce.

Conclusion

After examining the responses of the mothers in my study, we have to conclude that no work status is a Holy Grail. Full-time and part-time employment as well as being at home full time can be very frustrating; each can also be extremely satisfying.

Full-time employment is cited as very stressful because you can become exhausted managing the logistics of the demands from home and the office. Your sources of satisfaction from full-time employment are often the tangible rewards of a job—money, promotion, benefits, prestige, power, as well as experiences that build self-esteem and feelings of confidence.

Part-time employment is both frustrating and satisfying for the same reason. You can experience a lot of stress trying to meet the demands and needs of home and employment. The stress may occur because you find the expectations of home—because you are no longer employed full time—and the demands from the office—because you have responsibilities to the job—misguided and annoying. On the other hand, you may find part-time employment very satisfying because it allows you some time in the office which provides the intellectual stimulation, adult contact, and remuneration that are cited as frustrations of being at home full time. In addition you still have time—whether it is hours or days, to be at home and focus on your family.

Being at home full time you may well find yourself feeling lonely, wanting adult conversation, an identity other than mother and wife, and some money you can call your own. If you can be resourceful and think of activities that you could do to bring other people into your life while caring for your children, you may be less frustrated with being at home. The satisfaction you may well experience is most likely related to the reason you are home in the first place. You want to watch your children grow, be there for them, and expose them to the world while guiding them to be the best they can be.

Please note that although these findings are based on responses of many mothers, you cannot be generalized. You are unique: your circumstances at home, your education, your wishes, your relationship with your husband, your health, your work environment, attitude toward family time and your passions are yours and yours alone. Take this information as just that, information. Be aware of what these mothers thought. Use their information—think about their responses, while you assess your circumstances and values when deciding what work status is best for you and your family.

Chapter 4

What Is Parenting Anyway?

Parenting has become the catch-all phrase for child-rearing, caring for your child, nurturing, or raising your child. My question is: "What does all that really mean?" When the mothers in my study enthusiastically wrote how supportive their husbands—the other parent, the father of their children—were to them, they wrote such comments as:

> He does all of the cooking, and most of the food shopping (otherwise we split pretty "conventionally" along gender lines!)

> The only things I wish he did more was 1) learn to cook and 2) figure out how to do laundry so it gets clean (oh, and figure out that only human hands can fold laundry).

> He takes the children to dental and other appointments, makes meals, does laundry, buys groceries. He is helpful in driving our sons home from school and to and from other events. He doesn't take the garbage out.

These helpful activities of the fathers are important. No one would question and, I believe, most everyone would assume, that it is the responsibility of the parents to make sure food is on the table, the house and clothes are clean, and the children get to school, sport practices, or club activities, and all doctor appointments. In fact, these parental responsibilities are so pervasive and strongly felt that full-time and part-time employed mothers cited trying to do these tasks a main cause of stress in their efforts to balance employment and home demands. No wonder the mothers whose husbands stepped in—took care of some of these demands—are enthusiastic about this demonstration of support for them, their work status, and the family.

These very helpful activities and important activities are, nevertheless, tasks. Tasks that keep the family functioning and tasks that can also be relegated to another adult or even teenager. Parenting, however, involves much more than fulfilling these tasks. Parenting is about growing your children to be the very best people they are capable of being.

A huge aspect of parenting that goes beyond these tasks is awareness and assurance of the emotional health of each member of the family—husband and wife, each parent with each child, each child with the other(s), and the family as a social unit. Who takes on this responsibility?

Typically caring about communication, feelings, and behavior is a character trait positively associated with women—and women become mothers. The social movement in which both parents are employed and fathers are trying to understand and assume responsibility for the emotional aspects of parenting seems to be increasing. A book, *Getting to 50/50: How Couples Can Have It All by*

Sharing It All, by Sharon Meers and Joanna Strober (2009) skillfully addresses how to get to this ideal balance.

The following comments, mostly from employed mothers, suggest that their husbands are stepping in to do more than defined tasks. The quotes touch on the parts of parenting that are not tangible—communication, feelings, behaviors. This is the aspect of parenting that we, the parents, utilize in our personal skills to grow our children emotionally, socially, and psychologically. We need to communicate with our children by listening, expressing feelings, and modeling behaviors about how to 1) manage situations, 2) communicate all types of feelings, and 3) behave as responsible adults.

> We shared child-rearing…

> He's been a true partner, sharing the load in terms of housework… and supporting the kids.

> [He] worked with me on family, i.e., kid, problems. He has been a very active Dad, emotionally and in the car pool lines, and now is our primary caretaker.

As you can read, these quotes do not focus on tasks; they refer to something less tangible and obvious: "child-rearing," "supporting the kids," and worked on "kids problems," are words the mothers use to refer to the role the fathers assumed in the family that were helpful. What does a parent do to raise a child? How does a parent support a child? Solve "kid" problems? The answer to these questions is the essence of parenting.

According to human development research, we, human beings, grow physically, intellectually, emotionally, and socially throughout our lives. A child grows from a totally dependent baby into an independent, thinking adult. How does a dependent baby become an adult with all the qualities and abilities to live in our changing world? The answer starts with parenting. Parents are the ones who are the baby's first teachers and mentors. As a child grows, goes to school, visits homes of friends, interacts with other adults, makes plans for himself, he encounters other teachers, mentors and situations different from those he's experienced in his home. While these out of the home experiences undoubtedly affect a person's development, which is expressed in an African proverb "It takes a village to raise a child," and the source of Hillary Clinton's book titled *It Takes a Village: And Other Lessons that Children Teach Us* (Simon and Shuster, 1996), the parents create the foundation for development.

Although there is agreement about the role of parenting, how parents—mothers and/or fathers—assure the child's physical growth and encourage intellectual, emotional, and social growth varies a great deal. The differences are, once again, because the circumstances and values within each family are unique to each set of parents. Sometimes even the mother and father have different ideas from each other about how to handle a particular situation. How a mother[‡] behaves to convey values and ideas or "mold" behavior, is based on her assessment of

---

[‡] I have intentionally switched back to "mother" rather than parent or parents or mother and father because this book and study is based on information gathered only from mothers. I am aware and there is potential for a lot of discussion to include the thinking, behavior, and interaction that "fathers" brings to the role of parenting; just not in this book.

what is the best for her children. Similar to her decisions about her work status, how she interacts with her children is personal and unique to her and her family. While gossip often contains judgment on a mother's decision—"Can you believe she won't let...," OR, Can you believe she lets...?"—almost every mother's decision is founded in an effort to have her children grow up to be responsible, moral adults. Even though different circumstances sometimes require different rules and guidance, we often only know some of the situation. Would we then best display caution before jumping to a criticism of a mother's rules or behavior?

The seemingly simply goal of growing a child physically involves food. But, what a parent gives the child to eat: anything the child wants anytime, only organic foods three times a day with one snack at 4:00 PM, a vegetarian diet, or special foods because of medical needs of the child, can and does differ from family to family. How a mother manages the child's consumption or not of the food also differs in families and relates to what she learned in her own home—what the circumstances were and what she thinks worked and did not work when she was the child.

A friend of mine was employed in a home in which the mother insisted that the children have only organic home-prepared foods at all times including school lunches. This required at least an extra hour of cooking to prepare foods for the children's lunches. The only snacks allowed were vegetables or what the child did not finish at dinner the previous night. The mother had very strict rules because she wanted to be sure that her children had a healthy intake of food at all times.

Other families bow to the narrow palates of their children with the desire that they at least eat something. I once met a family whose children would not eat much beyond hotdogs and plain spaghetti. The mother brought suitcases filled with special food for the children lest they go hungry. She also brought vitamins to supplement the lack of nutrition in the children's self-selected meal plans. This woman's priorities were that her children at least eat something and she would address their health needs through vitamins.

Even though the "menus" are different, each mother is definitely trying to make sure that her children are healthy. She is also teaching them about conflict between what they may want and what mother wants; the children are learning how to get or not get what they want and the risk of not pleasing mother. How each mother handles disagreements at mealtime differs between families. It is very complicated. Parenting is not only what we do—what foods we have them eat—but also how we do it—how we enforce our choices.

How we discipline, how we enforce or choices, what and how we teach our children about themselves and others, how to handle the world, how to achieve, is based on: 1) how responsive we are to our children's needs—do we run to save and protect them; do we let them make choices and experience the consequences? And 2) how demanding are we about their behavior—what are our expectations about their abilities—what we believe they are capable of doing and what we want them to do?

Based on observations and interviews with many parents in 1967, Diana Baumrind, a psychologist, identified three parenting styles:

1) Authoritative—low responsiveness, high demandingness, i.e., "you do as I say";

2) Authoritarian—moderate responsiveness and moderate demandingness, i.e., "you follow the rules with our guidance and support," (this is message is not verbalized but implied by parental tone, attitude and, if needed, consequences to undesirable or disappointing behavior);

3) Indulgent—low demandingness, high responsiveness, "anything you want, you can have or do."

In 1983 researchers Maccoby and Martin added a fourth parenting style:

4) Neglectful—low demandingness, low responsiveness, an absence of parental attention, direction.

I do not think any of us are always one parenting style but if we think about our general approach when talking with our children, we tend to lean toward one style more than another.

Reflecting on my own parenting style, I think I mixed authoritarian with a bit of indulgent whereas my husband mixed authoritarian with authoritative. I remember when our first child was about 16 or 18 months old and was not the world's greatest sleeper. He really was not interested in going to sleep before midnight. My husband had had it, I was exhausted, and with the doctors' encouragement, we decided to let our baby cry and "learn to comfort himself" to go to sleep. One night we were lying in bed and our baby was in his crib in the next room. Soon we heard: "I want mommy. I want mommy." I was dying but willing to give our agreement a try. Then he said, "I want mommy in here now!" My husband responded with "Oh! He's talking in complex sentences!" I said, "That's it, I'm out of here. What's my boy want? Mommy's coming!" I was little indulgent, perhaps. I chose to do what was comfortable for me at the time. As our baby got older and could do more for himself, he did become one of the world's great sleepers; ask his wife.

I once encountered a mother with her three- or four-year-old son in a public parking garage who, I think, was trying to give her son a sense of empowerment. She, her son, and my husband and I were waiting for an attendant to bring our cars up to us. Her car arrived first. When my husband and I got into our car and were ready to leave the garage, I looked up to see her car blocking the exit. The mother was standing by the back door of her car talking to her son who was standing on the front seat facing backwards. The mother was reasoning with him trying to get him into his car seat. This went on for several minutes as more and more cars lined up unable to exit. I finally got out of my car to have an unasked-for chat with the mother. After confirming that I was sure she was a wonderful mother, I told her to just pick him up and put him in his car seat. This was not negotiable—he had to sit in his car seat! She looked at me with a big question on her face and responded, "Oh! You think he's older than he is?!" I thought, if he were younger, then even more reason to sit him in his car seat; no negotiating. It is the law and for his safety, not a decision he gets to make on his own.

Like my previous behavior, this mother was indulgent during that interaction—she was being highly responsive to his mood and not setting rules and guidelines for his expected behavior. Do we make a mistake when we think children need to have the power or decision? Are they sometimes asking for limits and testing us?

I do not know whether she was an at-home or employed mother and from the mothers' responses in my study, no parenting style belongs to any work status. As we will see, parenting style comes from both internal and external factors, but overwhelmingly it seems to be an emotional factor that relates to the personality of the mother and goes back to the idea of her values, choices, and what is important to her. Any difference between the groups is only intimated by their comments explaining their responses to the question: what have you learned about being a mother to your children over the past 14 years? There is not much difference among the work status group in what the mothers claimed they learned.

Looking at the responses of all the mothers, most of them (57%) wrote that they learned parenting skills: listen to your children, support them, treat them differently; each child is unique; let them learn from their mistakes. The second highest percent of responses cited by 17 percent of all mothers created a category on learning about oneself: I needed more patience; I should have been a better listener; flexibility is important. (*See* Appendix, Graph 5.) The comments from all work status groups contained references sometimes to parenting skills, sometimes to what they learned about themselves, and sometimes advice to other mothers based on what they experienced.

Some thoughtful comments from employed and at-home mothers about their personal learning frequently describe parenting skills:

> I've learned that what we think of as control is illusory. We can influence our children, but we cannot live their lives for them.

> I've also learned that their mistakes are not my fault. I can show them the way, but then they are responsible.

Also I've learned how different every child is, and that what works with one, does not necessarily work with the other.

I have "matured." My patience has increased dramatically. I've learned to accept my children as they are and not as I would wish them to be.

I learned a lot about loving and about being there, and many individual events: how to diaper, how to decide when to go to the doctor, how to comfort, how to get kids into colleges. But the hardest of all is how to let go and let them be (young) adults and to let them make mistakes, and to step back and let them be who they are, not who I expect them to be. It is really hard, but I am working on it, and I think I am getting there.

Mothers who commented below were employed in 2008 but mentioned their indulgent behavior when they were at-home moms:

I catered to them too much! Since I wasn't working, I didn't have any excuse not to wait on them.

We as parents tend to do too much for our kids and working parents do not fall as much into this trap.

Below, mothers bring up the quality versus quantity issue. All these mothers experienced employment and all value quality time. Some go further and note the worth of quantity too:

> Being a mother to my children has been the hardest, most challenging and most rewarding thing I have ever done. I have learned that children do not need quality time. They need quantity time. They need their mothers and they need them a lot. Children raised on a steady diet of nannies, day care and then after care programs are so starved for the kinds of steady love and nurturing that only a mother can give. I have also learned that compared to my career as a trial lawyer, mothering is much more demanding and yet allows for so much more creativity and requires so much more growth in me as a person.
>
> That it doesn't matter if I'm working or not—I could still give my children a lot of time, and "quality time" if I made time for it. And there were times when I was home all day and could get wrapped up with chores and other tasks and not focus on the kids.
>
> I have learned that the quantity of time is important but having the children feel they can connect/contact/converse with you if they want to is most important.

> [I] think once I stopped work and took more control over the kids' upbringing, was better able, both logistically and creatively, to encourage the two younger ones to pursue their own interests. If a parent has time, he/she can do more of these things to help their kids experience more things and become accomplished at one or two of them. If we had kept going at my previous pace, I'm not sure the younger ones would have gone down these (musical) paths partly because my husband wouldn't have supported these paths since they are totally outside his experience. I grew up playing classical piano, while he grew up doing sports.

These two mothers mention the subtle confusion a mother may experience when she questions her motives—is she doing something for her children or is it really for herself?

> It's impossible to distill (heck, it's impossible to know fully) everything I've learned. Lessons that come to mind include distinguishing what I'm doing for whom. That is, when I go out of my way to do something "for my family" or "for my children" . . . is it really for them? Sometimes I'd put lots of energy into things like special meals or activities that were special to me when I was a kid, and I really was motivated by love and a desire to do something for another family member or for all of them. But I've

learned to consider what THEY want when I'm "doing for" them. If they do not care one way or another that I baked this pie instead of nuking microwave brownies, there might be no sense doing it. I still might do the pie, but if I do so with the understanding that it's for my own fulfillment and not just "for others" I avoid the disappointment that is inevitable when I put more caring and energy into something than the recipients care about. Meanwhile, the kids' appreciation of some (by no means all) of the "special" things Mom does has grown as they've grown.

That's very much related to the old saying, "Do not sweat the small stuff." The difficulty is in determining what "the small stuff" is and what is really important. That learning goes on and on, but it was probably within the last 14 years that I identified this as an issue.

I've learned that I'm far from the best mother there could be, and probably far from the best mother there is, but I am usually confident that I'm the best mom for my kids (among actual existing people).

Each child has his/her own needs and what I thought they needed (my own unmet needs from my own upbringing) was not it at all.

Some of the next comments accentuate the modeling that parents do, contradicting the old adage: "Do as I say, not as I do."

> Being a good role model is equally as important as being there for them. As children grow up, they appreciate their autonomy and independence. Working allowed me to give my children some space. If I did not work, I probably would have been an obsessive and overbearing mom. Work helped give me a balance which I believe they have learned to emulate.

> Kids take their cues from their parents on how to cope with life's ups and downs. It's better to help them face the assorted setbacks instead of trying to "fix it" for them every time.

> My strength lies in helping my children to become their own persons, modeling such essentials as good decision-making and recovering from failures, and teaching them such truths as the fact that all relationships have conflicts, so expect them.

How we get involved and how involved we are varies in these thoughtful remarks below:

I firmly believe that close supervision, incredible amounts of love, advice, direction and support are crucial to raising productive and well-balanced children who will become great citizens of this world.

…that by being a mother there is always something you can learn from your child, that I am extremely protective of them, that I'm often concerned that they make the right decisions, that they are spiritual, intelligent and respectful. I'm proud of being their mother.

It is very important to stay very involved in what they are doing regardless of their laments that you should not on occasions. This involvement is far more important and of higher priority than keeping a very clean house or other traditional duties subscribed to mothers.

These busy mothers observed how important it is to focus on your children:

What I've learned is sometimes they need to come first, sometimes you and/or your marriage do. Parenting is like driving a stick [shift]—you need to have an intuitive sense of when to push, when to pull, when to ease off. The way my husband and I raised (are raising) them worked well for us and them. I am sure there are several other ways that would work well—like any endeavor; in parenting you need to play to your strengths and theirs.

Work always came second [and it] still does; that's the only way to raise children. You have to be available all the time and more so as they grow up. Actually, I sometimes think they need me much more now as they're getting ready to leave the house than they did when they were younger. The one daughter who has left only needs me when she's in trouble.

I was not willing to give up my career totally but I was willing to modify it. I also gave up a network of women friends for my kids. When time was precious, it always went to my family and then to my career. Friends came in last!

I think most mothers can identify with the feelings of frustration expressed by this mother. Bad days come to all of us. I suspect this was one of those days:

You can give them as much time as possible and they'll still want more. They seem to remember every activity you missed and forget or not recognize the extraordinary efforts you have made on their behalf. However, they are forgiving and loving and I think you just have to do the best you can and hope that they end up being happy and healthy.

These mothers thought the teenage years required more parenting than previously. Is that because they were experiencing the teenage years at the time of the questionnaire? Did they forget? Or were the teenage years just more difficult in their family? Any reason is possible:

> Now that my kids are older, I realize that in some ways, teens need you more at home than do little kids. I've also learned that basically, adolescents are like four-year-olds but with more technology and a driver's license. I've learned that the things you do for your kids that you think are important are often not the things they remember most. They watch and listen to the little things you do and say more than the pontificating and grand gestures. I've learned that the morals and ethics you teach your kids when they're young establish the basis for their character when they're older and out of your direct control. I've learned from my daughter that today's crisis is tomorrow's no- biggie. In other words, do not always get sucked into the emotional drama of the moment because it often will resolve itself. Better just to be sympathetic and listen without always trying to find a solution. It's also important, I've learned, to teach your children the tools to solve problems themselves

so that they have the confidence and the ability to do so without always turning to you.

It's HARD. I tried to create a warm, but structured environment for my kids when they were young. I could be tough because I knew that they had to learn how to be self-regulating, independent people...But I could not have imagined when my kids were young how hard it is to let go. Each of my children have faced challenges—some pretty difficult—that I couldn't (or shouldn't) help them with. I have had to let them deal with them independently. I have learned that what it takes to be a good mother changes over time—I have had to adapt to a different role—but my desire to be there for them and to help them and nurture them has not changed a bit. Being pulled between the two poles of letting them grow up and wanting to be part of their lives has been a great personal challenge for me.

Some mothers found that respect, which comes in many forms, is an important component of parenting:

I respected them. Even when I disapproved of what they did I told them respectfully. I think the respect I have shown them has boosted their self-esteem and has encouraged them to treat others respectfully.

If your child makes an error in judgment or strays off the desired path somewhat, just be there to help as best you can—but then move on. Never bring up past misdemeanors, do not nag constantly about issues that will eventually change (clothes, hairstyles etc.). Try to guide, not dictate. No one likes constant criticism or advice. When they come home, always cook their favorite foods for them. Big hit! I have learned most of all to let them be the person they want to be and not the one that I want them to be.

I've learned that all you can do is try your best to support them and love them and let them know you will always be there for them. I've learned how important it is to communicate with them, no matter how young (or old). I've also learned that they will each develop in their own unique way and even though you are the "same Mom" they react to you differently, based on their own personality and their own needs.

I've learned that they are hard to change ... so letting them be who they are is really important, and appreciating who they are is essential. I've learned you have to let go ... let them make mistakes and learn from them (hopefully) and love them just the same. I've learned (many times) that being angry doesn't improve any relationship and that "I'm sorry" are important words. I've learned (and am still learning) that being a good listener is often the most important thing you can do to help someone. I've learned that constructive criticism is hard to give and hard to get.

These mothers stepped back and looked at the time we have with our children and offer advice:

> One of the most important things is to talk to your children and listen to your children. It's amazing to me how much they heard when we thought they had tuned us out. Also, we need to let them fail and recover. Rescuing them is not necessarily a good idea. I have also learned to trust my instincts. My children tell me I have guided them in the right direction when necessary and they keep coming back for more advice. I find myself more and more saying "I really can't answer that for you, you'll have to make that decision on your own."

> They need age-appropriate independence and the freedom to make some decisions (even bad decisions). They learn through experiences and need to experience the logical consequences of their choices.

> You keep trying until it works. (Never give up) A support system of other mothers is invaluable for advice, sympathy and reality checks. I learned that

sometimes being a mother requires more patience and sanity than I thought I had.

And a mother who acknowledges the uniqueness of parenting techniques because each mother's situation is unique, her child is unique, and her values are unique:

If I have learned one thing it is that every child is exquisitely unique. What works for one, may not work for the next (or even ever again!) and that there is no hard and fast rule for any occasion. I have learned infinite patience and have known highs and lows with regard to my kid's behavior. Therefore, you can never judge another parent or parenting technique because each situation requires flexibility. I thought tantrums were the result of poor parenting until my beautiful fourth child rewarded me with one in Target when she was two. Had I only had three children, I may have lived the rest of my life thinking that tantrums were avoidable by just being a good parent! I go nuts when I read about "the perfect way to toilet train" or "the perfect way to get your child to sleep through the night" or "the perfect way to raise a teenager" because it is all so situation specific.

As you can see from the many quotes above, all the mothers, whether employed or at home really cared about their children. Their efforts to do the very best they could for their children are almost palpable. All mothers try very hard to be the best mother possible. Being a mother is hard, challenging, and filled with doubts. Flexibility about situations and behaviors may be useful to calm or avoid crises. Children are resilient. All mothers in my study—full-time employed, part-time employed, and at-home mothers—agreed based on their fourteen years of experience that if we listen, respect, model responsible behavior, love, guide, and let go when appropriate, our children will, we hope, grow to be happy, responsible adults. Our children will use their unique abilities, will love, and engage in the world.

I titled this chapter "What is parenting?" After sharing with you some of those things that are quantifiable such as providing for food, a home, education, transportation, and clothing, we know—and the quotes exemplify—that parenting encompasses a realm of more intangible things than it does tangible. It is a lifetime of loving, of giving 100 percent emotionally, physically, and personally to the happiness and welfare of another human being. Parenting cannot be quantified. Parenting is not easy but it can bring unbelievable, unmatched joy. We love, we give, we let go, and we try our best every step of the way.

Chapter 5

What Are The Side Effects Of My Work Status?

I trust that at one time or another you've read the small printed paper that is often stuck inside the bag with a new prescription. Along with drug chemistry information is the section labeled "Side effects." The side effects are usually negative and start out with annoying symptoms: diarrhea, constipation—take your choice..., weight loss, weight gain; and move on to ulcers, diabetes; and then go for the big ones, cancer, stroke; and sometimes death! If you took all this seriously, you would be crazy to take any drug. Luckily, most of these side effects do not occur and if some do, you know a possible reason and in consultation with your doctor, of course, stop taking that medication.

Actually, everything we do has side effects, not just medication and not all negative! If we go to dinner with good friends or family and have a really great time, we go home satiated and happy, and happiness is good for us physically and emotionally—side effects. If we complete a task and the project is well received we feel competent, others are complimentary and we are proud—all side effects. If we would not allow our son to take the car and he is angry, "family time" is apt to be less joyous as his participation has become monosyllabic—a side effect.

And, not all side effects are immediate and obvious—they could be related to long-time observations or experiences. I asked the mothers in my study how they thought their choice regarding work status affected: 1) their children's successes and/or challenges, and 2) what they did evenings, weekends, and vacations with their friends and family?

First, did the mothers think their work status affected their children's successes and challenges? Most of the mothers (66%) agreed that their children benefited from their work status. Many employed mothers noted that they were role models to their children—demonstrating the value of a good work ethic and how to manage a career and a family. They felt being this type of role model was good and important.

These mothers who were employed in 1994 and 2008 noted this benefit in many of the quotes below:

> If anything, my work status has helped my children see that they can be successful and happy if they do something they love. I think it fosters fearlessness about trying things, coming back from failures etc.

> I think I have been a positive role model for my daughter; sometimes she reminds me that I enjoy the challenges of work. My daughter has an excellent work ethic and looks forward to a career, although she is not interested in the kind of work I do for herself.

> I believe that it has served as a model to them that women can be very successful in full-time careers and have a successful family life.

One employed mother adds another dimension to the benefits of being a role model:

> I believe I've been an excellent role model for both my daughters to strive academically with career goals in mind. They see their mom and dad playing equal roles in providing and supporting the family. They have learned that men and women are equally capable and can accomplish successful careers. They have also learned to recognize each of our strengths and weaknesses and how my husband and I can work very well as a team to support one another.

On the other hand, at-home mothers could have claimed they were role models for staying home and demonstrating how to create a supportive, stimulating environment in which to raise children. Surprisingly, not one of the mothers originally or currently at home made such a claim in 2008. What a contrast to the 1950s thinking and values regarding being a truly feminine woman. The print media—newspapers, magazines, journals; television sit-coms, education institutions and corporations all espoused that women belonged in the home, society needed them to be not only their feminine selves, but to fulfill their biological destiny by raising their children to be responsible members of society. Women were also expected to create a warm and welcoming home for their children and husbands. "Move over Donna Reed" and "Hello Claire Huxtable"—progress for us! The print media, electronic media, our educational institutions, no longer create the 50s image of the little housewife at home in heels and makeup happily waiting on her man making sure he is comfy, relaxed, and happy. But, if we think for just a minute, everyone wants a warm and welcoming home, right?

The one at-home mother who alluded to creating this warm, supportive, nurturing environment wrote:

> We are blessed with very emotionally stable, well balanced kids. My husband and I both attribute this to our home being very emotionally stable and well balanced. The only way to provide that setting for our kids was for me to be home with them. If I were stressed with work, or with the schedule demanded by work, that setting would not have been possible.

Although the characters in the TV show "Mad Men," which recreates the male dominated life style of the 1950s men who work on ad campaigns on Wall Street, drink at least a two martinis lunch, and, of course, have many affairs starting with the secretaries in the office, might admit to valuing such a goal, creating a positive home environment apparently is not something mothers claim as an "achievement." Do at-home mothers not want to appear to value a lifestyle that is often belittled as "meaningless"? Do employed mothers not want to articulate they think it important because it is associated with traditional "women's work" in the home? Whatever the reasons, I believe we can agree that a secure, welcoming home environment is a condition we mothers aspire to create. We—and probably fathers too-- want our children to feel safe and to be able to use their energies to learn and grow; not to protect themselves against an insecure or volatile setting.

The only comment from an at-home mother that actually mentions role modeling, questions the benefit of her example to her children. Her concern stems from the practical perspective that economically it is very difficult for a family to exist on one salary and doubts her children will have her same situation. She wonders if her children would be more prepared if she had chosen employment, demonstrating how to combine career and motherhood:

> I do wonder sometimes, however, because I have only daughters, if my being home has been a good role model—as young women they may have been better served by a mom who did go out the door to work. The economics of their world may not offer the choices my generation has had and they may be better prepared for those challenges by seeing firsthand how someone strives to balance workplace demands and family life.

At-home mothers did not write they provided a role model for their children—it was not identified as a benefit of their work status. They did however, feel their chosen work status benefited their children because of a different behavior—they were available. The at-home mothers were readily available so their children could: 1) explore and participate in activities of interest and, 2) receive the emotional and educational support they might need.

These at-home mothers wrote about the benefits of being available to support their children's interests in various activities and give emotional and educational support:

> I think my stay-at-home status helped my children to feel loved, accepted and challenged to maximize their full potential. They had a rich, full childhood with lots of time for all the great advantages of family life. They were able to be involved in various activities such as Boy Scouts, church, family vacations, having friends visit, and yet were not raised "with a silver spoon"—having everything given to them. We were able to drive them to jobs when they were in their teens and they developed a great work ethic.

> Yes, in a positive way. One of my children was quite difficult—I had no escape and had to learn how to deal with her. I consulted with professionals and created a structured home environment that really helped and she is now doing very well. She also has a learning disability and I was able to help her a lot with schoolwork and get to know her teachers. This helped a lot. She now does well in college with no support and does fine in every respect. I wonder if I had been away more, if I would have recognized the issues. I think that being home was a positive factor for all my kids—but her in particular.

> I think my children have benefited because of the level of guidance and involvement I was able to give them by not being distracted by work outside the home.

Employed mothers made no such claim. However, like the one at-home mother who questioned if her non-working choice was a good role model for her children, they expressed concern about being available to give their children opportunities to explore diverse activities and receive emotional and educational support. "Availability"—being easily accessible to their children—was indeed important. These comments are from mothers who were employed full time in 1994. Some mothers reduced their working hours to part time, others created more flexible employment situations, and others decided to become at-home mothers:

> By working from home, I've been around for the challenging times and the successes.

> Being at home more as they got older (especially as their dad was away a lot) did help me become more available to them when they needed me—physically as a driver, errand helper, etc.; emotionally—I heard more of their stories, heard them talking to friends, was there and not tied up with work when they wanted to share; developmentally—I was able to do more activities with them, expose them to more things, explain and describe.

> My children were able to participate in many activities because I was available to support them after school and on weekends.

These employed mothers honestly question what being available would have meant for them and their children:

> It's possible that I've been less aware of things (situations, reactions, actions, emotions, I'm not sure just what "things") than I might have been if I were around for more hours of my children's days and therefore could have done more or done something more effectively to allow them to blossom more successfully.

> I believe that if I had been able to stay at home for a ten-year period when they were in elementary to junior high school, it would have been easier for them. Children like routines and when you work, it is much more difficult to establish routines.

Given the doubts of the employed mothers about the effects of the amount of time and how they were available to their children, like the concerns of the at-home mothers about role modeling, it appears all mothers—whatever their work status—are well aware of the important effects of both role modeling and being available to enhance the development of their children.

We love our children; we want to give them opportunities to explore activities and interests and we want to help them through challenges—help them think through situations and learn how to make decisions on their own. Some of the employed mothers claim their chosen work status enabled them to be good role models for their children. Some of the at-home mothers contend their chosen work status provided an availability to support the interests and development of their children. The employed mothers and at-home mothers claim their behaviors and their chosen work status bring different outcomes and benefits to their children. Both groups, however, are aware of and care about the benefits identified by the other group: at-home mothers care about role modeling and employed mothers care about availability.

Independence is another outcome both work status groups claimed they fostered. Yet, they gave different reasons. The employed mothers thought their children became independent because the mothers were not around to take care of everything for them. The children had to learn to do things for themselves. The at-home mothers thought their children became independent because the mothers were around, which gave the children a sense of security and confidence that enabled them to walk away and explore on their own.

Below are some quotes from the mothers who were employed in 1994 and employed in 2008:

> I do believe that my children's considerable successes in school and thereafter are a direct result of my not micromanaging their lives…My children learned such skills as how to plan ahead (because I didn't have the

time to run out to get supplies for projects), do their own homework and projects, and manage their time. These are life lessons that have contributed to their successes.

We didn't have time to "help" my daughter with homework and that was good—she learned to do it all on her own. Even my son, who needed more help, we had limited time but I think he got a lot of what he needed and the structure within which to achieve on his own.

They are in the habit of being places on time, with the right tools/equipment/books. They know how to use public transportation and get themselves where they need to go. I believe my working has contributed to their competence and self-sufficiency.

These quotes are from mothers who were at home in 1994 and 2008:

I also made my kids part of what I like to call "the home community." From the earliest age, they were folding laundry, setting the table, putting the toys away—with help at first of course and then on their own. I feel the time that I had to insist on these kinds of things have helped my kids be fairly independent and competent. My college age child regales me with the stories of all the students she meets who do not know how to do their laundry or cook basic scrambled eggs or pasta. I know a lot of mothers who seem to think it's their place to play with their kids and "give" them everything. Perhaps because of my situation with no family nearby and being almost a "single" parent with the kids meant that I expected more of them and they became more self-reliant. I really had no qualms with what to expect from children—drawing the line or laying down the law, when the kids were getting out of control.

Being a stay-at-home mother has allowed me the opportunity to teach, encourage, support, guide, help, watch over and enjoy my five children throughout their years at home. This has given them confidence and a great sense of well-being. All of them are independent and strong minded. They also have a feeling of stability and security knowing I am here for them when needed. I think being at home has enabled my kids and me to have close relationships.

I have heard it said: You either put the time in with your children when they are young, or you'll have to do it when they are older. I feel lucky to say that all of my children are very motivated, self-assured and independent. I believe it was the strong foundation and values I instilled in them by sharing my time and talents with them. All the skills I learned at school and [when I was] in the work force went into their development, a baby-sitter could not have accomplished as much.

Given that both employed and at-home mothers believe their children achieved independence as a side effect of their work status choice, it suggests that when we are asked for a reason, our responses—however sincere—serve to support our choices. Also worth noting, is that all mothers want their children to become independent. And, many of the children, can and do, according to their mothers, become independent people.

Like some of the employed mothers who questioned whether not being available to take their children to activities or to "be there for them" impacted negatively on their children, some at-home mothers wondered if being so available to their children had the ill effect of making them less independent.

These originally at-home mothers in 1994 contemplate the effects of their availability on the independence of their children:

> I think my children had some difficulty when I returned to school. They were used to me being available for them and I wasn't. I think they did become more independent and self-reliant, but maybe I want to see this to justify my going back. I do not think I can ever be certain.

Would our children be more independent or self-sufficient if I had been at work more? Perhaps.

It's given them a sense of security, but probably made them less independent than they would otherwise be.

This at-home mother chastises her own behavior for enabling immature behavior—continuing dependence on her, just because she is available:

> Accepting responsibility is our children's biggest challenge. Sometimes, my availability has enabled immature behavior. Ex.: One of our children has trouble getting up in the morning and catching the bus. Since, I'm not working and more flexible, I enable that behavior by taking her to school.

The following comment offers a perspective on micromanaging, sometimes thought to be a behavior of at-home mothers which, like availability, impacts independence in a child. One mother noted that micromanaging was not necessarily related to work status but to a mother's interest:

> I do believe that my children's considerable successes in school and thereafter are a direct result of my not micromanaging their lives, as all too often happens with moms who over-focus on their children. (I recognize that these moms may or may not work

outside the home—it has more to do with whether they have their own interests and activities other than their work status.)

If we continue with this thinking, then a question arises about the occurrence of micromanaging our children. Do some mothers micromanage because: 1) they are at home and do not have enough "other things" to occupy their minds and energy; 2) their personality is one that likes control and perfection; or 3) they want to put some order in their lives to lessen the chaos? Are some mothers helicopter parents because they need more to do "other things" in their life? Maybe this is true for at-home mothers. And, maybe a desire to "lessen the chaos" is a need most prevalent among employed mothers. If these hypotheticals can be answered in the affirmative, then we can conclude that either work status is very capable of micromanaging.

If one work status does not foster independence in our children over another, then what is the influencing factor? Once again, as is true of parenting, the mother's assessment of her situation and her values—what she considers important and how she communicates that—plays a critical role in growing children to be independent, confident, and responsible adults.

While role modeling was a beneficial behavior of employed mothers and availability was a beneficial behavior of at-home mothers, and both groups claimed their work status choice enabled independence in their children, what were the side effects of their work status on family and friends, vacations, and free time?

The highest percent of all the mothers in my study—36 percent—thought their work status was a good choice for them and their families—another example of how we positively rationalize our decisions. Most of the mothers—33 percent of employed mothers and 45 percent of at-home mothers were satisfied with how their work status choice affected their children and family life style.

The next highest percentage (27%) acknowledged they had no time for friends or family and were stressed. As you might guess, employed mothers comprise most of this group, for they are the ones who mention how stressed they are trying to balance the demands of employment with the demands of motherhood/family.

The largest difference between the employed mothers and the at-home mothers in 2008 is in the category labeled "no time/stressed." The employed mothers (34%) overwhelmingly compared to the mothers at home (6%), are too stressed trying to answer the calls of employment and their own family to have time to readily reach out to friends and other family members—siblings, parents, cousins. (*See* Appendix, Graph 6.)

One quote from an employed mother shares her realization that we all—all mothers and families—regardless of work status, have our struggles even though it may seem on the outside that life is easy and smooth.

> Talking with other working moms, I've seen much agreement with the sentiment we feel that we're OVERWHELMED much of the time which is stressful and happiness-defeating. Between work obligations, running a household, trying to meet all the kids' needs, and struggling to make ends meet financially, it just isn't easy. But also, as I've gotten

older I've realized that EVERY family's got its issues, and no matter how harmonious and together-seeming other families may appear, it's very likely that they've all got their difficulties/complaints, just as I do!

Interestingly, an examination of all three work status groups in 2008 shows that mothers employed part time were even more stressed than those who were employed full time. This difference between the groups is very small—only 2 percent—and it certainly is not significant. However, I do wonder why even a few mothers would find part-time employment more stressful because the part-time employed mothers objectively have more time for friends and family. Is part-time employment sometimes even more stressful than full-time employment? Is there something else going on that could contribute to the discrepancy, however minor?

The chart below shows that 72 percent of the part-time employed mothers in 2008 were at-home mothers in 1994 compared to 28 percent of the full-time employed mothers. Is it then more stressful to enter the workforce and reorganize your life with friends and family than to continue with what is familiar—being employed full time focusing mainly on your immediate family—children and husband? Is it the change in demands rather than the demands themselves that causes stress for these part-time employed mothers?

Percent of Mothers within 2008 Work Status

		Work Status 1994		Total
		employed	at-home	
Work Status 2008	FT	80.0%	20%	100.0%
	AT-HOME	6%	94%	100.0%
	PT	*28%*	*72%*	*100.0%*
Total		48.0%	52.0%	100.0%

These mothers, who were at home in 1994, commented on the limiting effects of their employment status. Part-time employed mothers wrote:

> I end up doing business work on evenings & weekends.

> Yes, I now go shop on weekends & Friday nights. I am useless. But I relax more on weekends too.

Full-time employed mothers wrote:

> Sometimes I have to say "no" to something I am asked to do. Sometimes I would reschedule my work so I could do something with friends and family outside of work. I have tried to work in an environment that is family friendly and allows for flexibility.

> I had more time for family and friends when I was a SAHM. Now that I am self-employed, I work constantly, sometimes having to wait days before returning a friend's phone call and have had to miss family gatherings too.

> When I was a stay at-home mother, I had much more flexibility as far as getting together with friends or going on trips. Now that I am working full time, I cannot be as spontaneous, but I still make an effort to do things outside of work and to maintain my friendship.

Some now-employed mothers cite the demanding schedules of their children or husbands as the impediments to getting together with friends and family or going on vacations, not work status.

> I do not think my evenings are affected by my work status as much as by my kids' activities. My schedule is dictated by their activities.

> What we did in our free time was dictated more by our children's status than work—i.e., sports, school schedules, etc.

Both employed and at-home mothers thought vacations—what they chose to do as a family in their free time—was an area that reflected the economic effects of their work status or their spouse's income. A few at-home mothers have a similar observation when they mention the ease of scheduling vacations because they just had to work around school vacations and their husband's schedules—they were free. The quote below exemplifies this:

> Because I wasn't working, we could more easily take vacations during the school vacations. It made our ability to take vacations much more flexible.

> With respect to vacations, obviously, we really only have to work around my children's school schedule and my husband's job.

Employed mothers often mentioned their ability to take wonderful vacations—expose their children to special places and experiences. A benefit of their work status was to have the money to be able to pay for such ventures:

> We've always managed to take special, memorable domestic and exotic overseas vacations as a family.

> My work status allowed us to afford things like nice vacations, so that was a positive aspect.

And some at-home mothers mentioned the effects of less income on their vacation choices:

We have taken fabulous family vacations, but maybe we could have afforded even better ones with an additional income.

We have not taken many vacations due to the expense and the few we've had are memorable. One year we asked our children "if you could go anywhere at all where would you like to go?" and the answer was to "visit family out west."

It is interesting that none of the at-home mothers even mentioned fabulous or exotic vacations even though we all know of some families in which the mother is at home and the family does take "special vacations." Perhaps the mothers do not see that privilege as an effect of their work status but rather having sufficient income from their husband's employment or other family resources?

If we look at the "bigger picture" of these side effects, what activities a family chooses to do when they are not doing their "jobs"—school, the office, or tending to needs of the household and its members, we encounter another aspect of parenting.

I know of several families in which both parents have professional careers that require advanced education degrees and the children are excellent students. Each member of the family is so busy doing his job that few activities outside the home are done as a family group. The children are not often exposed to cultural activities such as sports events, movies, museums, theater, opera, or other states or countries. All members work hard and respect the efforts of each other. Other families take every opportunity to introduce their children to every cultural activity "advertised." And other families spend vacations and free time with extended family members, friends, and neighbors.

Imagine the different messages and exposures the children receive in each of these three different types of family behaviors. Think about how these experiences impact their development and choices in their employment, social interactions, and life style as they grow to become adults.

Yes, again, financial situations and family schedules are factors that affect these behaviors AND values—what is important to us, also influences our decisions about vacation and free time choices.

Looking back at the original two part question: 1) how has your work status affected your children's successes and challenges and, 2) how has your work status affected your time with friends, family and vacations, can we draw any conclusions? Does one work status affect children and free time differently from another?

Yes, according to the comments some mothers chose to write, there are some differences. Employed mothers, feel that: 1) they are positive role models to their children about how to combine employment with motherhood and, 2) they are often exhausted and stressed from employment and home demands so they have little or no time for friends or extended family, though they sometimes are able to take more "exotic vacations." At-home mothers note that 1) they are available to enable their children to explore interests and activities, and readily receive educational and emotional support, and, 2) they are not stressed as they would be from demands of employment and have flexibility scheduling time with friends, family, and vacations.

The differences claimed by both groups, however, are not from all the mothers and are not black and white. Even more important is that mothers in both work status groups were keenly aware of the importance of being available to provide opportunities for their children to have diverse experiences as well as the importance of "being there" for them. Similarly, many mothers—employed and at-home—valued independence in their children. Although each group acknowledged different behaviors—ones compatible with their work status, which resulted in independent children—they both valued and sought the same outcome.

Mothers care very much about the impact their choices have on their children, work status being one. Mothers try very hard to give their children the tools to become responsible, independent adults. The choices we make to achieve these goals depend upon our circumstances and our values. As seen in these responses, there were differences and similarities but the goals and concerns were similar; we try, we care, and there are others out there who feel as we do.

Chapter 6

Why Do Mothers Change Their Work Status—Or Not?

Most employed women do not know—really know—how they are going to feel about full or part-time employment until they have delivered the baby. For some women, having that baby changes everything, including work status. I know it did for me.

When I did the research for my dissertation in 1994, the 103 at-home mothers had not always been at home. Only one percent—one person—never was employed. She gave birth to her first child just after she finished her Ph.D.—definitely work—just not the paying kind called "employment." (Unfortunately, she did not participate in my follow-up study so I do not know if or when she re-entered the workforce.) As we know, motherhood changes "everything."

The largest group of mothers (60%) stopped working to stay home "near the birth of the 1st child." Some mothers plan on staying home before they become pregnant. Others find they just cannot leave their baby with someone else, and others realize it does not make sense to return to employment because their salary will all go to childcare—what is the benefit? (*See* Appendix, Graph 7.)

As I mentioned earlier, I assumed I would remain employed at least part time after my first child was born. However, the funding for my position was cut so I would have had to look for new employment and I did not have a pull towards a career. I became an at-home mother—so much for another assumption!

I recently met a mother who stopped teaching junior high in the inner city so she could stay home with her baby. Although she missed her students greatly, she concluded that her students were troubled because they did not have a consistent adult in their lives. How could she then leave her own child? We all have slightly different scenarios, but our decisions come after careful thought. Once again, and always, we consider our situations, values, and what we think is best for us and our family.

Almost all of the employed mothers (95%) in my 1994 study continued employment after their children were born. Probably most of the full-time employed mothers took the maternity leave allotted by their employer but they generally did not extend their time home. (*See* Appendix, Graph 8.) It is interesting to note that 80 percent of the mothers who were employed full time in 1994 were employed full time fourteen years later, in 2008. (*See* Appendix, Graph 9.) These mothers were relatively consistent about maintaining employment.

I used the terms "relatively consistent" and "employed full time" because, during those fourteen years, 46 percent of the employed mothers indicated that they had changed their work status. Some of them did change their work status: several switched to part-time employment for a few years, others were out of work for some months, and some took a leave of absence. While these were, indeed, changes in work status, others claimed they changed work status when what they really changed were their employment conditions.

These quotes are comments from mothers employed in 1994 who changed their work status:

My firm offered a generous buyout package and I was feeling burnt out after doing the same thing for 15 years. Plus, my daughter had junior and senior year of high school ahead, both of which are very stressful, and it seemed like a good time to devote my attention to her. As my husband said, "Why would you wait until she's out of the house to leave your job, why not take the opportunity to give her your undivided attention with college apps and exams coming up?"

Preliminary note! I didn't make a putatively permanent change in status, but I did take a 5-6 months' leave (including some vacation time and about 4-5 months of leave without pay). I felt pulled just a little too tautly and needed some sort of a break. The biggest thing I missed being able to do with the work-home juggling was being involved in my kids' lives and schools, and that was both a reason for taking the break and one of things I was able to do more of while I was on break; what really prompted it was a more non-rational sense that I was getting too miserable and needed to stop and breathe awhile. I felt I was missing out on some of the mommy-ness I wanted to have, and wasn't feeling particularly "fulfilled" in my work.

From the time my third child was born in 1990, through the time I quit work in 2001, I was constantly torn between a never-ending job and never having enough time for my family. I continued working for financial reasons as I was the sole support of our family. When I left it was a combination of being tired of long work hours, always feeling stressed and exhausted, and realizing that I needed to be more in touch with my kids as they started their middle school and high school years.

These mothers who were employed in 1994 remained employed but changed conditions about their employment situations:

I changed from an administrative position to a faculty position so I would have more time with my family and because I was interested in the type of work.

I changed jobs in 1998. I left a company to join a company in the same industry for several reasons. The new company was only three miles from my house, so I had no commute. The workload at the previous company had become overwhelming and all my colleagues at my management level left the company in a short time leaving me with their projects, staff, and clients. I was looking for better balance.

I developed a repetitive stress injury, and could modify my home work space better than my at work workspace; it helped my husband for me to be at home, because his father lives with us; I needed more time with the children, so there were several reasons to have a job where I could work part of the time at home.

Perhaps some of these mothers who changed employment situations rather than work status felt such relief from the stress of trying to be more available to their family, they experienced their new employment as if it were a new work status—pressures were reduced significantly. Whether their change was status or situational, by far the largest reason they gave for changing their status was because of their children (77%). Contrary to the stigma some of society places on employed mothers, these mothers certainly care about their children!

Many at-home mothers (58%) also cited children as a reason they changed their work status but, like those who cited "fostering independence in their children" as a side effect of their work status, their reasons are different. Rather than wanting to spend more time with them, the at-home mothers thought their children had grown enough—were at school during the day, so they no longer needed to be home all the time.

Below are some quotes from at-home mothers regarding changing their work status:

> I wanted to stay home with my children and I did until the younger was in kindergarten. For financial reasons, I then worked part time while they were in school, but I was there at the close of school and resumed being at home.

I was ready to add another dimension to my life as my children got older and went back to get a Master's degree in library science. I thought that this would allow me to work part time as a law librarian, allowing me to utilize my law degree...without having to enter into a stressful, most likely full-time career. I went to library school in the evening when my oldest was in middle school and able to manage her younger siblings for an hour or so until my husband got home. I finished library school and got a part time job when my youngest was in fifth grade. The hours were flexible enough to work out fine with his schedule and those of my older children.

I felt I needed to work on a career so I would have something to do as my children got older and left home. I needed to have an identity outside of mother and wife.

I was able to work once my children were all in school. I would not work if they would have been in daycare, latchkey, etc. I have four children to put through college!

In addition to feeling that they no longer needed to be home all the time for their children (58%), these resourceful at-home mothers planned ahead and sought employment to have more money to pay for college (55%) and to do something for themselves (45%); something they found personally satisfying.

What about the mothers who stayed in their 1994 work status? Although slightly more mothers did change their work status—or employment situation, 49 percent of the mothers stayed. It is no surprise to discover that having a career—job promotions, success—was the primary reason employed mothers maintained their work status. Nor is it surprising that children—wanting to be there for them—was the primary reason at-home mothers maintained their work status. Both career and children were the passions each of the mother groups identified as a driving force behind their initial work status decisions. Clearly fourteen years later, these passions continued.

Given that employed mothers do care very much about their children, they supported their continued employment by saying they had excellent childcare or were able to provide financial security and health benefits for their children. At-home mothers cited finances too but for a different reason. They felt they could remain at home and still have financial security and health benefits because their husbands earned enough. Once again, all mothers want to make sure their children have a stable environment and security. They make different choices to provide these circumstances but it is important to both groups.

A few quotes below give some texture to employed mothers' decisions to remain employed. They clearly espouse enthusiasm for the interesting challenges of employment and appreciation for the financial effects giving a nice life style, personal independence, and money for retirement:

I enjoy my career. Also, I want financial security in retirement. I have 30 years with the federal government and the pension benefits which come with that service.

I knew that I wanted my children to have a solid education and attend a private school, therefore maintaining my job was important. I advanced my degree in order to advance my career. I enjoy working it provides me with self-satisfaction and a level of financial independence.

I became an academic at (local university).... I made the move so that I would not be traveling a significant amount, would have a more flexible schedule, and could spend more time with my children. The move came at considerable sacrifice financially; my salary at the outset dropped by 50 percent. (Several years later), my husband left the family....and I was not in the frame of mind to change jobs at that point. Although the above points sound grim, I should also make clear that this job is constantly rewarding and I feel incredibly lucky to have it. So, the initial financial sacrifice and the subsequent negative reasons for sticking with the job pale in comparison to what a good decision the transition was for me.

The at-home mothers write about their passion for taking care of their children and, like the employed mothers, also mention finances, but in a different context. The at-home mothers state that they do not need to seek employment because their husbands make enough to take care of the needs of the family:

> When my husband died in 1994, I was profoundly grateful that I was able to keep on being a stay at home mom. The last thing the kids needed was further upheaval in their lives. I had a network of friends who helped look after the kids during his 8 month battle with cancer (I'm not sure I'd have had that network of at home moms if I'd been working) and we were able to keep the structure of our lives after he died the same: mom is home and she will look after you. Fortunately, I have not had to go back to work, which many widows do. Advice to stay at home moms: make sure your husband is insured!!

> My middle child had serious medical/learning problems which caused me to need to stay home to care for her as well as my other two children. She had many doctor/therapist/tutor appointments and my children were born very close together. Finding affordable, reliable, responsible childcare was impossible.

I decided not to go back to work because my husband's job was so demanding of his time and his travel schedule so erratic. We felt that the children needed one parent they could count on always being in town. Financially, my husband made enough money that I didn't need to work.

What can we conclude? Some mothers (51%) change their work status and some (49%) do not. Both work status groups say that their children, financial situations, and a sense of personal pride, impact their decision about their work status.

Spending time with their children is a reason some employed mothers may choose to reduce, take a break from, or change employment conditions. At-home mothers may choose to stay at home so they can continue to be available to their children or choose to find employment because they feel that their children are away at school more and do not need them to be at home as much. Whether or not the mothers in either work status group change their status, all want to be available to help their children grow to be the best people they can be.

A financial concern is another factor that impacts our decision about employment. Some employed mothers remain employed because they feel their family needs their income to support a desired lifestyle, college, and/or retirement. Some at-home mothers, however, elect to re-enter the workforce when their children are still at home because they want to earn money to help pay for college tuition and/or save for retirement. Yet other at-home mothers gauge the family income—their husband's income, family money, or saved money—as enough to pay for college and retirement. Consequently, at-home mothers, depending on their assessment of their family's financial situation, may change their work status...or not. The bottom line is that being able to support our lifestyle, whatever that may be—pay for college, if that is one of our values; plan for retirement—are all financial situations that affect our work status decisions.

A sense of personal pride is another factor that may influence our employment status decisions. Some mothers sought employment because they valued financial independence and were very proud of their ability to earn enough money to be independent from their husbands' incomes. Others chose employment because they wanted an identity beyond mother and wife. At-home mothers, on the other hand, did not talk about financial independence creating the sense of pride both groups sought; they just wanted to "be somebody" in the professional world so valued by our society. A sense of personal pride is, actually, important to all of us: according to the mothers in my study, two forms of personal pride emerged. One, financial independence, was derived from employment success, and the other, a professional identity, was obtained by seeking employment outside of the home.

All of the factors: children, finances, and sense of personal pride are considered by mothers when we assess our current situation and our values regarding our choices about employment and what we think is best for us and our families. These factors clearly played a part for the mothers in my study regarding changing their work status...or not.

Chapter 7

What Are The Challenges?

The saying "if you have your health, you have everything" is often associated with older people because they are the ones who often have health problems. As we age, our bodies begin to fail us from wear and tear. We want to be as we used to be or like everyone else—it is challenging to have health problems. But there are other causes of poor health besides age, which can affect any of us. When we, someone in our family, or a friend is not in good health, the "if you have your health, you have everything" saying takes on a whole new meaning. More to the point, it really begins to mean something pervasive to us. Managing any illness is demanding physically and emotionally—it is exhausting, challenging, and often stressful.

Unfortunately, of the mothers in my study who commented that they had challenges, more than half (54%) of them said they had health concerns in their family that were challenging to them. In 2008, the highest percent (62%) were the at-home mothers who wrote that "several family members had physical or mental health problems." The second highest (42%) were the employed mothers who cited "parent illness or death" as extremely challenging/stressful. When I examined the responses closely, I found that many of the "several family members" included "parental illness and/or death." (*See* Appendix, Graph 10.) The takeaway from this is that as we and our children grow, our parents age too. We become the sandwich generation responsible for the care not only of our children but also of our parents.

Becoming the sandwich generation brings many issues to the forefront. Let us just examine what happens when your in-laws become ill. First, who takes responsibility for their care? You? Your spouse? Both of you? Second, are your in-laws nearby or in another state? Third, are there any siblings around that can and will help and not add to the concerns by expressing differences of opinions about what to do? Fourth, do you know your in-laws' insurance for health? Long-term care? What about a Living Will or Power of Attorney? The answers to all of these questions affect the degree of challenge and worry we encounter when we find ourselves suddenly caring for our aging parents. If you honestly think about answers to any of these questions or the many dynamics that could play out, divorce might begin to look like a good option!

I can remember when my father-in-law was suddenly a widower. At a loss how to cope, eventually we moved him near to us into a retirement community. We did the legwork—finding a facility and relocation together as well as visiting and socializing as long as he was mentally capable. As time went on he had mini-strokes, which eventually impaired his functioning so that he had to be moved to a nursing home. My husband definitely took the major responsibility for handling the complicated finances which were frustrating and confusing. The nursing home would say one thing, Medicare would say another, and his bank account said "not much." Eventually, over months, it was all ironed out. I, on the other hand, seemed to be the one who did more of the visiting and dealing with any hospitalization and the nursing home staff. It was not fun and I recall on occasion thinking to myself, "He's not my father..."

As mothers we often assume that the nurturing and caring for others is our responsibility. Some of us do not think that way; rather we assume that male and female parents can both nurture. Saying our spouse is "helpful" suggests that someone else—hmmm ...the mother?—is in charge. Whatever the current situation, traditionally nurturing was considered a positive female attribute. We are trying to share this quality; the question remains: are we there yet?

My study shows that employed and at-home mothers are greatly concerned with a physically or mentally sick family member—assuring proper care for that person is important to both. Given that at-home mothers do not have the time demands of employment, they frequently do a lot of transporting or visiting the "patient" and handling of medical and care issues, whether nearby or in another state. Employed mothers find themselves trying to find time in their employment/home demands to attend to the needs of an ill parent or child—definitely very difficult for them too.

When I was in elementary school, my mother decided to enter the workforce. I remember a conversation she had with her mother about her new work status, employment, and thus, lack of availability. She assertively told her mother that she could no longer take her to places or appointments because she had a job. My memory is that my mother was very pleased that employment protected her from being at the beck-and-call of her parents and in-laws. I might have made this up...such is the nature of memories.

The comments below are from mothers who were at-home in 1994 and 2008. Their experiences with health issues among family members seem overwhelming:

> We had a miscarriage and in the following year experienced the death of our son from a long term illness. My husband suffered from depression for a period of time. My husband and I experienced the loss of our fathers and helped our mothers downsize and relocate.

> In addition to my husband, my mother-in-law died. She was senile and our responsibility and I had to spend a considerable amount of time tying up her affairs. My dad developed dementia and my mom moved in with me that year. My dad has had to go into assisted living which has been a financial strain while I sell off their property to pay for it.

> My mother died…after a brief, rare, terminal illness; my youngest child spent several months in residential treatment for substance abuse, and is doing well, but this is extraordinarily stressful; my husband suffered a mild stroke… but has fully recovered.

These quotes from mothers employed in 1994 and 2008 show that health issues in their families are of great concern and very stressful to them too:

> My father died of pancreatic cancer. We had to help my parents for the 18 months he was ill. My mother was killed in a car accident. I had to administer her estate…and clean out her home.

> The ongoing challenges of a son that suffers from clinical depression and an aging parent for whom I supervise a caregiver team 24/7.

> My daughter… was diagnosed with depression and an eating disorder. We dealt with this for the better part of three years, including having her in a full time residential program. This was probably the single thing that absorbed our family the most during that time. Then, two years ago, I was diagnosed with breast cancer and went through surgery, chemotherapy and radiation. It was very hard. But our family had been through a lot already, and we faced this together. I leaned very heavily on all of them—my husband and two children, as well as my extended family and friends. And I continued to work as much as I could throughout the cancer and treatment—it saved my sanity to have something else to think about. But there were times when I was just laid out.

Mother died of cancer and I had to travel frequently to... assist with care. Sister died in of cancer and lived out her last few months with us.

As the above quotes from at-home and employed mothers demonstrate, if we or family members experience physical or mental health issues we can expect challenging and stressful times. Not only does the adage "if you have your health you have everything" appropriately express the sentiment of the "patient" but it makes the saying "life is not a bowl of cherries" take on a reality for mothers when thrown into this new care-taking role.

Another challenging health issue identified by the mothers in my study was the appearance of ADD/ADHD in their children. What is ADD/ADHD? ADD stands for Attention-Deficit Disorder—inability to focus, easily distracted. ADHD stands for Attention-Deficit/Hyperactivity Disorder—cannot sit still, impulsive behavior. You can, however, "forget" the term ADD because since the 1994 version of the *Diagnostic and Statistical Manual of Mental Disorders IV*, commonly known as *DSM-IV*, the symptoms describing the behavior: Attention-Deficit Disorder (ADD) are now a subtype of Attention-Deficit/Hyperactivity Disorder with predominance on the inability to pay attention and less on the hyperactivity. The term ADD officially is no longer.[§]

[§] With that distinction noted, the National Health Institutes Survey conducted by the Center for Disease Control (CD3) in 2004 -2006 asked parents if their child had Attention Deficit Disorder (ADD) or Learning Disorder (LD) or both. Given that since *DSM-IV* (1994), the term ADD has been recognized as a subtype of ADHD—not a separate disorder—and Learning Disorder (LD) is a separate diagnosis in the

ADHD is a prevalent diagnosis and is growing. According to a Center for Disease Control and Prevention report Increasing Prevalence of Parent-Reported Attention-Deficit/Hyperactivity Disorder among Children—United States, 2003 and 2007, (2010):

- The percentage of children with a parent-reported ADHD diagnosis increased by 22% between 2003 and 2007.
- Parents report that approximately 9.5% of children 4-17 years of age (5.4 million) have been diagnosed with ADHD as of 2007.[**]

Of the mothers who reported their children have learning challenges, 72 percent of them were diagnosed with ADD/ADHD. The percentage of children from my study (8.2%) is pretty consistent with the national statistic of 9% mentioned in the above report. (*See* Appendix, Graph 11a.)

Some of the quotes below shed light on struggles mothers experienced trying to help their children be successful learners.

At-home mothers in 1994 and 2008:

My son has inattentive ADD. He is an easy-going bright person so it wasn't identified until he was in 8th

DSM, it can make discussion and statistical patterns difficult to assess—we aren't always talking about the same symptoms.

[**] While parental reporting gives higher numbers than the numbers based on a diagnosis by a medical professional that includes dispensed medications, the mothers in my study did the reporting; I have no way of knowing if their child is or was on medication.

grade. I have read many books and articles which state that kids with ADD benefit from having a full-time at home parent. It gave me encouragement for my choice to be available to my children first.

Several children had reading and concentration problems. They have received some treatment from a visual therapist.

My son struggled initially with dyslexia at school. For years he attended a tutor which I believed helped a lot. However, when he went to (another country for)...high school, we did not ask for any special treatment for him.... He is conscientious and so is prepared to study. ... I think he would have been embarrassed to have been given special consideration at school as a new boy in class and indeed he managed without it. After all, the workplace affords no such considerations.

This comment was from a mother who was at home in 1994 but employed in 2008:

My elder son is on medical leave from college, after effects of over- prescribed medications for depression and wrongly prescribed meds for ADHD (did not have it).

The comments below from mothers employed in 1994 and 2008 identify learning problems and also mention some emotional concerns:

> My son had some rough times in school (starting early/mid elementary), probably related to mild ADD and related social difficulties. It's actually a continuing issue, and I've wondered and researched to try to determine whether some of the issues he has are remediable. ...he surely spends way more time on his homework than his peers do, and way more than his teachers intend, and the product does not reflect the time spent.... And he isn't interested in putting any time or energy into determining whether there might be strategies that would help him be more successful or efficient at getting the work done in the longer term, so things just go along. I haven't been able to let go of this "there must be a better way," yet I would not force the issue, either. (So, emotionally, I guess I'm taking it out on myself.)

> Both sons have ADD and significant problems with school achievement; my daughter does not. Both sons have issues with depression; my daughter does not.

> My daughter has learning disabilities that are challenging, but not profound. From first grade through 9th grade, she attended tutoring once or twice

a week. Through constant attention to this issue, we have managed to overcome her most serious problems, although she remains a fitful student.

An interesting finding was that 80 percent of the employed mothers, compared to 55 percent of the at-home mothers, claimed that they have children diagnosed with attentiveness learning challenges. Why are 25 percent more employed mothers reporting children with ADHD? (*See* Appendix, Graph 11b.)

An examination of the educational demographics of the mothers that are associated with the occurrence of ADHD in children provides some relevant information. The demographics of the identified families in my study are different from the national demographics for families with children with ADHD. Nationally, most children diagnosed with ADHD have mothers whose highest level of education is high school. In my study, only 2 percent of the mothers fell into this demographic group. The education level in my study of most of the mothers with children with ADHD (73%) fell into the nationally second largest category—mothers with graduate degrees. A closer look shows that of those mothers, 85 percent were employed compared to 33 percent who were at home.

Why would the employed mothers who more frequently have graduate degrees (72%) than at-home (48%) mothers, have more children with learning challenges—ADHD? Are highly educated people—never mind mothers—more aware of potential learning difficulties? Do they more readily see the struggles in their own children? Are they more motivated to quickly identify problems and obtain the resources provided?

Perhaps the different lifestyles between the employed and at-home mothers play a part in the percent of ADHD children reported? Do the employed mothers have less personal time to spend the extra hours apparently needed on homework? Do they seek outside help more readily because their schedules are so tight? Can they—more than the at-home mothers—afford the professional help? Or, do their goal-oriented attitudes associated with their being employed,[††] increase their drive to obtain the tests and resources available within the school system? Or, perhaps employed mothers found ADHD a challenge worth mentioning and at-home mothers did not.

There are other issues that arise when addressing the prevalence and causes of ADHD. One is that the reporting and diagnosis of attentive learning challenges is uneven—some are parental reports (this study); others are based on surveys from doctors who provide medication to children for ADHD.

Efforts to attribute causes of ADHD shed light on the confusion surrounding the diagnoses. A frequent discussion about ADHD is whether or not poor nurturing is the cause. Is your son (more boys are diagnosed with ADHD than girls) out of control and inattentive in the classroom because of poor parenting? Because of lack of discipline?

[††]

In my dissertation I compared the gender-related character traits of employed and at-home mothers. The term, gender-related, means that both men and women have a trait and the trait is socially acceptable BUT preferable for one gender. The employed mothers assessed themselves to be significantly higher on every masculine trait than the at-home mothers assessed themselves. Conversely, the at-home mothers assessed themselves to be significantly higher on every feminine trait than the employed mothers assessed themselves. Goal orientation is a character trait more frequently and positively associated with men. Consequently, I would expect that the employed mothers may tend to demonstrate more goal oriented behavior than at-home mothers.

Or, is there a brain chemistry disorder causing his inability to focus and sit still? I will ask another question: is your child inattentive or very active because he is immature for his age and prefers to play rather than sit, listen, and learn small motor skills?

A good friend of mine was concerned that her son had ADHD because the teachers in his school said he was disruptive in the classroom—not paying attention, and not reading at a level he was capable of doing. As time went on, the concern grew and they asked his pediatrician, who concluded the boy tended to be hyperactive and inattentive. More tests were done with a specialist and eventually the boy was put on medication. Yes, his attention in school improved and according to my friend, he lost his fun and happy personality when on the medication. Over the summer the whole family moved to a new location and they took the boy off his medication for the summer. The new school thought he had delayed reading skills, worked with him, and his attention and learning took off. Was it timing? Misdiagnosis? Impatience by teachers and school officials because he was disruptive in class? Hard to answer but the concern that ADHD is disruptive to learning is real; whose learning—the child's and/or other students in the class? How can we really know?

Although only a small percentage (10%) of the mothers identified mental or emotional concerns as a major health issue of a child, their comments reveal that becoming a mature, confident adult in our society is difficult for many and often requires professional assistance:

Comments from both employed and at-home mothers are below—they are "the same:"

> My (child) is still on medication for depression and anxiety, under the care of a psychiatrist. It is working well....

> One child has a unique learning style and often has test anxiety. One child was diagnosed as having major depression while at college, still under treatment after returning to college.

> One teenager has difficulty with controlling anger. Requires lots of work on the parents' part to help deal with life's problems

Health issues have a huge impact on a family. These issues can be generational—finding ourselves taking care of our children AND at the same time the declining health of our parents. Health concerns can also focus on learning struggles of our children or, more positively put, assuring our children enjoy and feel competent in an academic environment. And, we may find ourselves buoying a confused or depressed child to discover or rediscover a sense of competency, pride, and enthusiasm for pursuing interests and embracing adulthood/life. Although the comments of the mothers do not offer "how to" or "what to do" answers, they tell us that to have health problems and confront them is challenging, exhausting and stressful. We meet these challenges because that is what we do. It is hard. But it is important and we are strong.

As mothers, we face many challenges—not just those related to health. Employment concerns can be another source of stress. When both mother groups commented on stress they felt was related to their work status at any time since 1994, they identified similar employment issues.

Ironically, although balancing demands of work and home is definitely seen as the most frustrating aspects of full- and part-time employment, only 24 percent of all the mothers who wrote about stressful aspects of employment mentioned employment/home demands. Another 24 percent indicated they experienced stress trying to get back into the paid workforce. More mothers (36%) wrote about problems with supervisors or co-workers causing tension and worry

Below are a few quotes expressing their stressful employment problems. The first two are from employed mothers. The last two are from mothers at home in 1994, but who re-entered the workplace:

> I had a difficult work environment for many years; a co-worker that I had to share projects with was a difficult and unpleasant personality. I worked hard to find ways to mitigate problems. I sought help from my immediate supervisor and upper level superiors, but with no success. I even tried conflict resolution strategies and seeing an Ombudsman. Eventually, I did the only thing that I could do to eliminate the problem and the stress: I changed careers and jobs. Someone else in the office filed an official grievance against her as she was making life difficult for most people she supervised.

> Working full time –the difficulties with the supervisor drained me emotionally.

I found it much more difficult to re-enter the working world than I anticipated. Having management experience made me "over qualified" for entry-level work (probably a euphemism for "too old to work" next to 22-year-olds) and yet having not worked in the field for 15 years made me unqualified for anything but entry level work. I experienced mistreatment by employer ...

After being a stay-at-home mom I had to make some real adjustments to working full time again. I am very glad I did not have to make those adjustments when I had babies or small children at home but it seems there are never enough hours in a day with a full-time job, responsibilities of motherhood...

Sometimes personal situations were causes of stress, although not a very large percentage—25 percent of at-home mothers and 13 percent of employed mothers—wrote that they "questioned themselves or their employment." These quotes below contain feelings of inadequacy that we women recognize and sometimes admit we have. In any case, these feelings do not make us feel good and take up energy so we have less to give to others—starting with our children.

(I had) periodic feelings of unfulfilled promise/inadequacy for not pursuing paid professional work or building a career, having a "real" business card or professional identity at receptions and dinners.

Working in my husband's office was a constant stress—I didn't like it at all since I had been home for so many years and was not up to speed on the things they did but I was thought to be up to the task. Fitting a few days a week work in with zero support at home felt very stressful to me with the kids so young and everything else going on...

The decision to remain part time v. switch to full time was an issue for many years. I missed the opportunity to pursue manager jobs (and move up the ladder) because of my decision.

I was more or less forced to change jobs, and it has not worked out that well for me, in fact. I feel I've had a "crisis of confidence" that leaves me struggling with feelings of insecurity on the job, on and off.

Some of these feelings we bring on ourselves, but they do not come from nowhere. These feelings often stem from our interpretation of what society (others) expects or views as valuable. We choose to feel inadequate because we think we do not "measure up."

In his memoirs, former President Bill Clinton talks about being selected to be a Rhodes Scholar—the most prestigious international scholarship awarded to students to study at Oxford University in

England. Upon first meeting his co-students, Clinton was very humbled and wondered how he got to be selected to be among these very intelligent and able people. At the end of the journey, after spending time with many of the others, he wondered how all of them were selected....

While I am getting better, in a charity or planning meeting I am still often hesitant to say something or ask a question—I do not think I know enough and fear sounding stupid or irrelevant. This feeling is based solely on the fact that I did not have a career and did not become "somebody" in the workforce. Consequently, these meetings are unfamiliar territory and I do not belong to "the club." I fear there are rules and information I do not know. Over time I have discovered that many people do not ask questions and some pretend they completely understand when, in truth, they hold the same fears I have. When I ask my questions, sometimes it turns out I am asking a question many others have too but have not dared to ask. We do best to trust ourselves, our instincts. So what if we do not know—if we knew we would not have asked. What is wrong with not knowing? Do we, perhaps, cause problems when we pretend to know?

From the quotes below, written by both employed and at-home mothers, instability in the employment of either parent, or in the marriage, causes stress. Sometimes the stress is about finding time to care for the family and other times financial problems occur which are always stressful.

> My husband, (after he retired went to another job that took him to different states during the week.) We did not move to join him. He kept a separate apartment (in

each of the states) and came home on weekends. This lasted for almost six years, with my taking all responsibility for our children during the week. As the only parent at home during the week ... it was very difficult for me to take business trips, and we had to work around my husband's schedule.

I have had to make changes in employment over the years, mainly to raise my salary to stay in the same house and have the same income for my family that alimony and child support had afforded me. As alimony and child support has stopped, I have had to squeeze my budget to make ends meet and change jobs to make more money. Conflicts and stress are a natural byproduct of a working mom, single or not. It is a balancing act that sometimes works well and other times is a struggle.

One reason I returned to work was instability of my spouse's job. He then stabilized his employment & started traveling more, so I decreased my hours. Some of my work hours made me unavailable to my children. With my husband traveling, (it) was a concern.

According to the responses of the mothers in my study, the types of challenges and the stresses they experience are not, for the most part, associated with one work status or another. Both work status groups experience the challenges and stress that occur when they find themselves responsible for the well-being of their parents or in-laws. At-home mothers may more frequently be involved in daily activities caring for a parent that is local because they are "available" during the day and an employed mother is not. Employed mothers find themselves stressed rearranging schedules and trying to manage logistics to address these same problems. At-home and employed mothers are challenged and stressed by the complications of being in the sandwich generation—it is not easy, it is exhausting, and stressful. If we cared less, it would be easier but that is not who we are. We are nurturers.

Both employed mother groups reported that they had children with learning problems diagnosed with ADHD. Although the percentage of employed mothers with ADHD children was slightly higher—though not significant—than the percent of ADHD children reported by at-home mothers, the reporting and diagnosis of children who struggle with attention or impulsive issues is too inconsistent to assess any association with work status. Emotional or mental health concerns of children were also extremely stressful for both employed and at-home mothers. The responses of the mothers revealed no difference related to their work status. What their responses did show is that the sayings "if you have your health you have everything" and "life is not a bowl of cherries" are all too true. The families in my study live real lives, filled with challenges and stresses to meet and handle according to both their values and their assessment of the situation. Like most people, they try to do the very best they can for themselves and their families.

While not all challenges cause great stress, there are other "typical" situations that happen in life that can and do cause a great deal of stress to those of us who experience them. The mothers in my study identified stress caused by problems with supervisors or co-workers, efforts to get back into the work force, disintegration of marriages, reduction in finances, unsteady employment, and employment situations that create feelings of inadequacy. There were no differences related to work status except that the employed mothers wrote more about problems with supervisors and at-home mothers wrote more about the challenges or obstacles to getting back into or being a part of the workforce.

We mothers, while taking care of our families, also try to use a little of our energy to take care of challenges that confront our families—maintain a steady home environment for our children, and find or continue opportunities to feel good about ourselves. We can start by making sure that we take time for ourselves. If we are over stressed, feel alone, frustrated, or exhausted, then we do not have the energy to give to our children or handle the many challenges in life. If we make sure to take care of ourselves—no matter how selfish this may seem to us, if we feel good about ourselves then we have the positive energy to reach out and care for others—care for the members of our family, our children for starters.

Chapter 8

Can We Really Have It All?

Colin Powell, in his autobiography *It Worked for Me: in Life and Leadership* (2012), tells how his family keeps him humble. Upon receiving a promotion in the armed services, he proudly goes home wearing the uniform that embodies his new and important career position. When he walks in the house his then teenage daughter looked up from her home work and shouted to her mother: "Mom, the GI Joe doll is home!" Just in case he lost perspective—had grandiose thoughts about his promotion—his daughter abruptly brought him down to earth. He came into his home in the role of career man, displaying his recent success, but to his daughter, he was still "just" her father, another role he assumes in life.

The term "role" can have different meanings in addition to an acting part in a performance production. One refers to different attitudes or behaviors of a person such as the role of "good cop" versus the role of "bad cop." As mothers, some of our behavior roles are: disciplinarians (good cop and bad cop), cheerleaders, comforters, as well as moral advisors. "Role" can also refer to the many tasks or functions we assume within a role. Mothers often function as chefs, chauffeurs, teachers, coaches, pet trainers, schedulers, doctors.

We are not actually chefs or chauffeurs, according to society and the Department of Labor. We are not financially compensated for preparing meals or driving the children to appointments—nice thought, though! Nor, do we receive performance reviews, promotions, or awards for our work—another good idea! In addition, the term "role" refers to the different social roles we assume, which are defined by the relationship and responsibility we have with others. These roles can be familial ones: mother, daughter, wife, aunt, grandmother, in-law; relational: friend, co-worker, neighbor; or positional within a group: employee, volunteer, part timer. In my study, I use "role" to mean the different social relationships and responsibilities we have towards others in our lives. I also discuss behavioral changes that occur over time.

We all have different roles in our lives all the time. In my questionnaire, I asked the mothers about their assessment of their social roles of mother, wife, career woman, friend, volunteer and daughter. I wanted to know if, in each of the roles, they felt they received recognition for their efforts: experienced satisfaction; felt competent; and whether or not the role utilized their abilities. As mothers we take on, or not, these different roles in our lives when we have young families. Each role brings different challenges, demands, and relationships. How well do we feel we handle these demands? Do employed mothers differ from at-home mothers in their assessment of themselves? How do the different roles make us feel about our "whole self?"

In 1994 the mothers who were full-time employed assessed themselves differently from the at-home mothers regarding the amount of recognition and satisfaction they felt they received in the career role. Their assessments were significantly different.[‡‡] Further, both groups also assessed themselves significantly different from each other on how they felt about their volunteer roles. They rated themselves differently on the amount of competence they felt, how comfortable they were, and whether they thought these roles used their abilities and brought out their best qualities. On the scales that were significantly different, the initially employed mothers felt better about themselves, ranking their response higher in the career role than did the at-home mothers. And the at-home mothers felt more positive about themselves, ranking their response higher in the volunteer role than did the employed mothers. This finding is not surprising because the employed mothers were the ones who had the "career" role as viewed by society—employment outside the home. The at-home mothers typically did more volunteer work at their children's schools and in the community; they more readily had the time.[§§]

[‡‡] A scale was created for the mothers to assess how they felt in each role. For example, the mothers rated from 1 to 5 (not very/none to extremely), the degree they felt they received recognition in the role of career woman. They did this for all the roles: daughter, friend, mother, volunteer, and wife respectively. They did this assessment again for each of the feelings or perceptions they had regarding the competence they felt in each role, comfort, satisfaction, and the degree the role brings out their best qualities and abilities. A mean was calculated for each scale on each feeling or perception and each role for the employed mothers and then for the at-home mothers. These means were compared and a statistical t-test of independent means was done. They were significantly different at .05 level—most at the .01 level. This means, for example, that there is some factor contributing to the different valuation the employed mothers gave of the recognition they received in the career role from that of the at-home mothers; the different assessments are not due to chance.

[§§] Also, in 2008 when I asked them to rank their feelings related to their career role, not all the originally at-home mothers thought they had a "career role" as an "at-home mother" so either did not respond or gave themselves a very low ranking on all the career scales. It is also worth noting that both groups did feel positive about themselves but employed mothers had consistently lower means than the at-home mothers in all roles except the career role.

These few quotes by mothers employed in 1994 illustrate their positive assessment of themselves in the career role:

> I continue to grow in my business ventures and am more confident about what I can accomplish in that arena. I am not as insecure in social situations where profession is the topic.

> I was a bit worried jumping back into practicing law after being out..., but it only took a couple of months to feel competent and confident again.

The valuation of the originally at-home mothers in the career role is not so positive but was not all bad either:

> I was out of the workforce for too many years—so I suspect that I will always have some degree of insecurity.

> I think that because I have not been a career woman I have put all my time and energies into the other four roles and feel it has brought out my best qualities and abilities.

The following quotes from at-home mothers depict their positive assessment of their experience in the volunteer role:

> I have done many things as a volunteer and have a lot of skills. So, I feel very competent as an individual and believe that I could get many jobs if I chose to pursue them.

> Volunteering has always been a positive for me but I can't remember any accolades in my other roles.

These quotes from employed mothers do not perceive their volunteer role as highly:

> I think some things have suffered over the years as I have gotten busier and put in jobs of more responsibilities: I used to sing in my church choir, which I no longer do. I do not volunteer much anymore; I use the weekends to rest and be with my family.

> My volunteer work at my children's school has changed from my being very active to my doing very little. This has been my choice—I had to give something up, and I felt it more useful in terms of building friendships to volunteer when the children were young.

Another interesting difference is that the employed mothers rated themselves significantly lower in the role of mother than the at-home mothers rated themselves. The difference appeared not only in the comparison of the 1994 work status groups on feelings of competence, but also in a comparison of the groups in 2008 on the scales: of recognition received, competence felt, comfort in the role, and feeling they used their abilities and the role brings out their best qualities. Why would at-home mothers consistently feel more appreciated, competent and comfortable in the role of mother than the employed mothers? Is this yet another example of positively supporting our choices—at-home mothers chose to be at-home mothers, therefore they feel better about themselves in the role of mother—rated their feelings higher? Or, are the employed mothers less satisfied and feel less appreciated and competent in the "female/homemaker" roles because they spend less focused time in the role? Do they feel guilty? Do they believe that society infers they should spend more time in these roles and thus, they have doubts about themselves?

In addition to the scale ratings, I asked the mothers to write a comment if their feelings changed about a role since 1994. For two of the roles—mother and career woman, several mothers from both work statuses wrote about changes that occurred over time. After fourteen years, some mothers were not happy with their role:

> I do not feel like I am a good mother anymore, as I am not able to help my children learn sensitivity, they cuss me out and disrespect me all the time.

> I'm finding it difficult to adjust to being a mother to two young adults who are out of the house. The

transition has been difficult. They need a different kind of parenting which I'm still trying to figure out.

And, some mothers, 40 percent, wrote that they felt more competent in the role of mother once their children had grown. They also noted that their children expressed appreciation to them which had not been forthcoming before... there is always hope. These two comments summarize some positive reflections:

> The feeling of competence in the role of mother has changed and improved when it comes to my oldest child who had emotional difficulties. During her difficult years I definitely didn't have the same feeling of competence that I do now that she has improved. There were many days that my husband and I felt we must be to blame for her problems. Now that she is feeling better she has told me how important we were to her during her most difficult times.

> As my children have grown up and 2 have moved out on their own, I have developed a feeling of satisfaction that they have grown up to be responsible, hard-working, moral young people. I feel that all the effort put into being there for them and nurturing them to the best of my abilities has been very worth the effort. As a full-time stay-at-home mom one of my most important roles I always felt, was raising my

children to be intelligent, well-rounded and moral, godly people. Intensive parenting is rewarding.

The following quote summarizes the ups and downs many of us experience in our familial roles:

> It is hard to compare being the mother of small children, daughter of healthy parents, wife of still striving to make it husband to what I am now. I have seen some sad and scary things since then- I'm not the same person. I feel both less competent and more competent at the same time. It is hard being the parents of young adults—it is not always comfortable at all, but is wonderful at times, too. I feel that over these many years, I have tried very hard to be the best wife, mother and friend that I could be. My relationships are the most important things in my life—by far—I get the most satisfaction and most challenges from them. I could not have imagined how trying, at times, it can be to "launch" your children into the world. Ironically, although my job is fine, my real passion is the people in my life. That is much clearer to me now than in 1994.

Launching children brings up another aspect of roles—roles change over time. "Once a mother always a mother" is true, we are not the same kind of mother throughout the course of our children growing up in our home. We switch in some of our functions and certainly in our behaviors. These changes come about subtly so we often do not notice or articulate the new experience and feelings.

I can remember when our first child went off to college, I felt a hole in my stomach; when our second child left I was sad but also felt free. Why the difference? I definitely loved and valued both. Thinking about it, I realized I no longer had to be home at a particular time, I did not have to drive anyone anywhere and I did not have to worry where someone was… when they would be home. I could meet my husband and go to the movies anytime; I had time to do anything I wanted—within reason and a certain freedom became evident and welcome. The difference in the feelings from first to second child's departure was simply when the first child departed, I was still in the "mother" role with a child—true, not children, but still a child, a dependent. We were still a family. I had a child to care for, prepare dinner for, daily interact with and help to continue to grow to be a strong, proud, confident person and…someone (my first child) was missing—the hole in the stomach. When the second child left, all those daily responsibilities left too. Both children, of course, were missing from the home and I missed them, but as long as they were happy, I could enjoy the change in my home; it became just the two of us (and the dogs); that is a different environment. My mother role had shifted.

I had different functions and daily responsibilities. It was time for me to really start letting go of my children, another behavior I had been practicing increasingly as they grew, made their own decisions, assumed responsibilities, and incurred problems. I knew this was going to be bigger and harder because they were setting out making their own lives. I wanted to be there for them, to support their efforts, to offer counsel, but not interfere with their choices and decisions. When our functions change in a role, we need to adapt our behavior.

I asked the mothers to comment on what role or circumstances they felt best utilized their capabilities. According to the mothers in all work status groups, "launching your children" can be a very positive experience. In 2008, 60 percent of employed mothers and 63 percent of the at-home mothers wrote comments concerning growth of children and being freer. In other words, after their children left the home, they felt freer in the role of mother to expand their own interests and were better able to use their capabilities. (*See* Appendix, Graph 13.) This is what I experienced.

In addition to changes in familial roles, some of the employed mothers in the study commented on the unwelcome changes they were experiencing in their career role:

> There have been times in the intervening years when "career woman" would have had a higher rating.... I feel as if I may be winding down on the career woman front (whether this is a permanent trend or a phase, I can't say with certainty) and I haven't shone much in that role in recent years. A variety of circumstances contribute to this situation, primarily the nature of my work assignments and the HR and political trends in the office. (They are much younger—than older—worker friendly, with primary emphasis on making the generation y-ers happy. As most of us have observed in the U.S. generally, the workplace especially, older-unfriendly policies, practices, and atmospheres start

disadvantaging woman at a much earlier age than they affect men.)

My recognition as a career woman has diminished as I have gotten older. Younger males are climbing the ladder and replacing women like me. Lots of animosity among my male peers aged 60-ish. [There is] definite favoritism toward younger white males.

Although both comments above suggest problems at work in part because of favoritism for male employees, I have also heard from friends that working in a "younger office" can be very uncomfortable. There are not necessarily any policies. It is just the perception of the younger workers that are not welcoming. "You" are past your time and are not included in the social group. Given that social groups at work usually arise naturally from sharing common experiences and interests outside of the workplace, it is understandable that a mother who has launched her children would not spend much time socializing with women or men—that can potentially bring trouble—who are dating and contemplating marriage—or not. We can and do befriend people in different marital and parental statuses from our own, but we tend to bond more strongly with those who are similar to us.

In contrast to the frustrations cited by some of the employed mothers, some of the originally at-home mothers felt differently about their "career" or volunteer activities looking back over the fourteen years:

And while I do not have an official career, I have a great deal of involvement in many organizations. I've probably grown a lot in the career area as I got more involved with things, even as I was home with my family.

I actually haven't worked "outside the home" now for a number of years. I certainly could not/would not go back to what I had once done, but I have had so many community volunteer and leadership opportunities over these years, that I definitely feel competent.

The mothers also looked back in a more general sense in their responses to my question: What are you proudest about yourself as a person? Three categories emerged from their written comments: 1) accomplishments about work, their children or both; 2) personal growth, their achievements or strengths; and 3) character traits, roles, behaviors or personality they value. Not quite half of all the mothers (45%) described traits, roles, and behaviors they demonstrated or developed that made them proud of themselves. When I compared the employed mothers responses in 2008 with those of the at-home mothers, to determine if one work status group cited these personal qualities more than another, I found they were almost equal. The employed mothers (46%) and at-home mothers (42%) both felt they were proudest of their "personal traits and behaviors." (*See* Appendix, Graph 14.)

The similarity of their responses continued with questions about: 1) what they would want to tell professional people about themselves and, 2) what they would want to tell an old friend they had not seen in a long time about themselves.

Looking first at their proposed responses to a group of professional people, the comments fell into four categories: 1) achievements, degrees, titles; 2) where or how they have made a difference in the role of career woman or mother; 3) personal strengths, qualities that they have to offer others; and, 4) a little bit of everything—kids, interests, work, achievements.

Once again, predominantly all the work status groups[***] employed full time (35%), part time (42%), and at-home mothers (37%) wrote they would talk about the same subjects: achievements, degrees, and titles, when talking with a group of professionals. (*See* Appendix, Graph 15.)

It is interesting that the highest percentage from any work status group was that of part-time employed mothers and these were not the mothers who were originally at-home in 1994. A surprising 67 percent of the mothers, who would discuss their achievements and were working part time, were employed in 1994. Perhaps now that they were sometimes out of the workforce and in the role of at-home mothers, they felt the need to restate their claim to belonging to the workforce—accomplished women who were also mothers. This would support the fact that 100 percent of the mothers who were employed full time in 1994, but were at home in 2008, would choose to talk about achievements and professional titles when talking with other

---

[***] This time I chose to look at the three work status groups: full-time, part-time employed and at-home. I did this because further examination of who the employed mothers were who would talk about achievements, titles, showed an interesting, unexpected, composition which I wanted to, and do, discuss in the paper itself.

professionals. Did they, like the now part-time rather than full-time employed, feel the need to let others know they were competent people even though they were at home—no longer in the workforce? Were they in some way reacting to society's inference that at-home mothers are not very achievement oriented?

A few at-home mothers mention their accomplishments in their volunteer role:

> Just as they would talk about their careers, I would talk about how I spend my days—and the volunteer/board work I'm involved with.

> That I have a very impressive resume with leadership responsibilities through the many volunteer positions I've had.

A few part-time employed mothers who were employed full time in 1994 would discuss their areas of professional experience and expertise, e.g., attorney, political, "interested in working."

When thinking about the responses, it makes sense that the highest percent of mothers in each of the work status groups chose to discuss achievements when with professionals, because that response is socially expected and acceptable. In addition to giving responses that support our choices, which I mentioned in Chapter 5 on side effects, when both employed and at-home mothers thought a side effect of their work status was that their children were independent, we also are very sensitive to the "appropriate" responses—give desired content depending upon with whom we are talking in social situations.

According to Dr. Jean Baker Miller in her book *Toward a New Psychology of Women* (1976/1986), women—often in the subordinate role to the social values and behaviors established by men in our society—are extremely adept and "sense" what is appropriate to do or say in a particular situation.

Are we tapping into our subordinate and sensitive selves when we choose to discuss achievements and titles in professional gatherings—knowing it is the appropriate conversation that the once predominantly male population was interested in discussing? And, professional gatherings are always an opportunity to network, a behavior that women are increasingly trying to do for themselves in the workforce.

Are the professional accomplishments typical answers or are they tied with a demographic of young people, corporate people, and highly educated people climbing whatever ladder? I was recently with some friends from out of town and my husband and I brought them with us to a casual barbeque of primarily people in politics or journalism. Rather than staying at our side, they mingled easily with the other guests. When we left the party I asked them if they had enjoyed themselves—met some interesting people, had good conversation. The wife, a warm observer of people and dynamics, had a great time. She enjoyed listening to the "titles," international travel, political crises at the office. The husband, on the other hand, was annoyed by the name dropping, or degree dropping, or promotion dropping. He would have preferred a conversation about ideas. Was it the youth of the crowd at the party—those still trying to make it that brought this discrepancy in expectation of what good party conversation could be? Was it the competitive tone of the geographic—Washington, D.C.? Obviously, not everyone wants to talk about or hear about employment achievements, which means that the consensus of interest expressed by the mothers in my study is, after all, of definite interest.

I found from my experience with longtime friends, including those I have not seen in years, when women talk to women—particularly to longstanding friends—we typically discuss everything: the personal—children, self, marriage/relationships, then work, and then the future. This is exactly what most of the mothers in my study from both work status groups cited they would choose to discuss with a long lost friend—everything.

The mothers' comments emerged into four categories regarding their responses to what they would talk about with old friends: 1) children, family, or marriage; 2) definition or examples of what being a good friend means; 3) myriad of things about self, family, work, life, and the future—talk about everything; and 4) evaluation experiences related to work, home, or the future. As I noted above, most of the mothers (62%) indicated that they would choose to talk to an old friend about a myriad of subjects—everything. The second largest group (25%) focused on sharing about their personal relationships: family, children, marriage.

A comparison of the mothers employed in 1994 with those at-home showed that the largest percent of both work status groups—employed mothers (66%) and at-home mothers (59%)—wrote they would talk about everything—self, family, work, life, and the future, to longtime friends. (*See* Appendix, Graph 16.) This trend held true in an examination of the 2008 work status groups. The full-time employed (61%), part-time employed (53%), and at-home mothers

(74%)—the highest percentage in each work status group—stated they would talk about everything to an old friend.

A quote from an at-home mother, a part-time employed mother, and a full-time employed mother respectively about sharing "everything":

> Generally about my life.

> [I'd tell her] about the joys and sorrows I have experienced, how my family is doing, what I enjoy spending time doing, what I am reading and thinking about, my thoughts on the issues of today.

> That I am so grateful for the opportunity to raise a family and that I now look forward to a new chapter in my life now that my children are on their own.

Women and groups are complex; not every woman in every group nor every group of women actually talks about everything. Maybe in a one-to-one situation, which my question clearly implied, and the other is a sincerely trusted friend, then the conversation will flow honestly on most any topic of a personal nature. However, like our roles and our behavior in our roles, what we are thinking about and choose to share with friends changes over time. I know that when I first began to reunite with a group of friends from college most of the time was spent asking, "Do you remember...?" Sometimes I wondered if I was there—I did not remember. As time went on we would have side conversations about children, family; straightforward, but most everything was still presented in a positive light. As time went on, and we all experienced that "life is not a bowl full of cherries," our conversations became more honest and extremely supportive—accepting each of us where we are.

I know that I have reflected on the different aspects of my life and have evaluated what I have experienced, some "results," and whether or not I can say to myself that I am satisfied or happy with what I have done and am doing with my life. My status is I am very happy with personal life—children, marriage, friends, social life and experiences; perhaps less so with extended family. But the one aspect of my life I am not fully satisfied with is my professional/career life. Yes, I have headed up committees, been on community boards, and others, but I have never really used my intellectual abilities or challenged myself. Thus, I did my follow-up study to my dissertation—the topic a belated but true passion. Whatever does or does not happen with this body of work that I am creating now, so be it. What is very important to me is that I complete my study by formulating my thoughts into a package, so all is gathered together and the information is set down for others to think about, share, and feel good about themselves as they journey through the familial and social roles related to motherhood. I hope to take what we all know—what sits inside the back of our heads—and move it to the front, active part of our brains, for awareness, discussion, and planning.

What is the takeaway about our different roles in life and can we really have it all? From the responses and comments of the mothers in my study I think it is fair to conclude that all roles, as in life, have ups and downs. Some of the mothers who loved their careers became disenchanted with their experiences in the workforce near retirement.

Would they conclude they were not happy in their career overall? They were not successful? Probably not. Some mothers indicated that they were disappointed or were having rough times with their children. Would they conclude that they were not good mothers? Maybe at one time or another, but that is what ups and downs mean—sometimes things are great and we are happy, sometimes, faced with hard challenges, and we are not so happy.

I wonder if it is really such an important question: "Can we have it all?" Is a divorced mother who raised her children by herself and worked to support all of them able to say she had it all? Is an at-home mother who raised her family and then focused on her grandchildren able to say she had it all? Who is measuring and judging? According to whom do we have it all? Our neighbors? Society? The mothers who chose a different lifestyle from us? What is it that we value; what we are judging? Who "decided" having it all—the implicit social value behind the gold ring mothers are trying to capture—is being both a mother and a career woman? All can refer to other roles besides mother and career woman—what about friend, traveler, volunteer, opera lover, swimmer, gourmet chef or gourmet eater? And chief relaxer? Once again, personal values and personal choices come into play. We are the only ones that can evaluate our contentment and satisfaction with our roles.

We do best in our different roles if we are prepared and aware of what we are doing, the choices we have, and what challenges and changes are in the future. Then we can say—and no one else—if we have had it all.

Chapter 9

Who Gives Us Support?

I was talking with a doctor about whether or not her husband was supportive of her in the care of their children—an 11- and 9-year-old. She confirmed that he was very good and that they had learned to work together over the years. She said that when the children were babies, she would be up early—very early and very tired—getting the children ready for daycare before rushing off to her medical practice, while her husband was sound asleep with his head resting nicely on his pillow! This annoyed her just a little. Finally, one day she asked if he could get one of the children. To her pleasure and surprise, he said, "Sure!" and hopped out of bed and took care of the child. After that he would sometimes ask, "Can I help you?" and her response was, "No, I have it!" Musing over her "stupidity"—not letting him step in—she noted that she was raised to think that taking care of the children was her responsibility. It did not matter that she was also a doctor; they were her responsibility. Now, she claimed, she is learning and so is he. If he asks if he can help and she invokes her ingrained sense of responsibility, he often will respond, "I know you have it, but can I help anyway?" She now says, "Yes!"

I asked the mothers in my study two questions about the support they received from their spouse. The first was *if* he was supportive and the second was *how* he demonstrated his support.

Support can come in many ways, and I was interested to see what kinds my mothers chose to mention if, in fact, they felt they received support.

In the above scenario, the support the doctor's husband gave was for the tasks that need to be done for babies—dressing, changing, bathing, feeding, burping, rocking, and playing. By stepping in to tend to these needs of his child, he was also supporting her by recognizing what she is doing, respecting her efforts, time, and profession by taking some of the chores on himself. Consequently, she was receiving physical and emotional support from her husband. If he just sat and watched, read the newspaper, or kept his head on the pillow, she might begin to feel less like an equal and more like a maid. If our husbands tell us they will take a night feeding because they know how exhausted we are, they are supporting us—our feelings and our efforts. If our husbands pay for us to take classes to further our education or to fulfill an interest, they are supporting us financially and psychologically—they know something is important to us and they step in to make sure we are able to "do it." If they say to us that they are concerned about a child's frustration with school, ask what we think, and indicate they will take steps to help our child; our spouse is a true partner. He is a liberated and sensitive male—allowing his "feminine side" to show because he cares about the emotions of our child and he is sharing our sense of responsibility for the development of the whole child.

Most of the mothers, 88 percent, responded that their spouse was supportive of their work status. But, when the mothers were asked how their spouse demonstrated support over the years, 32 percent of the mothers—the largest category albeit by a small margin—described a lack of support: "we are separated/divorced"; "my spouse isn't thrilled with my work status" or "my spouse is a little selfish—doesn't seem to value all that I do." (*See* Appendix, Graph 17.) Why the discrepancy? Why would 88 percent say their husbands were supportive but then a third of them write that in retrospect, they were not supportive? Could it be that initially or for a long period their spouse was supportive, but looking at the dynamics now, he could improve?

The comments below capture the frustration mothers felt about the lack of spousal support.

An at-home mother in 1994:

My ex (husband at the time) was not supportive of helping out with appointments or caregiving when I worked. His job was always more important than mine, regardless of my stress levels from having to do it all.

An employed mother in 1994:
My difficult work situation drove him to the brink, especially when I brought my work problems home. I know he would have preferred me to stay at home with the kids.

The second highest group, 30%, in the category labeled "Ok with what I do," has comments that range from just "okay" to he is "wonderful and very supportive." The observations below illustrate the weak support these mothers felt they received from their husbands, although most others felt full support.

An at-home mother in 1994:

My husband was content with my work decisions and [yet he] also doesn't consider it a real job either.

An employed mother in 1994:

I do not know whether he "gets" my need to be around and do the mommy stuff more than working full time would allow, but he at least intellectually understands it (I think) and he accepts it. He didn't actively support my taking leave without pay for a few months, but acquiesced and did make an effort to be supportive.

Below, the more frequent and enthusiastic quotes from mothers in both work status groups.

Typical comment from an at-home mother:

Yes, he believes strongly that I should be at home focusing on home and children. [He] is extremely supportive. When money is tight he's ready to brainstorm ways to save or make more money. He would be supportive if I chose to go back to work, though he believes strongly that the best place for me is at home full time. He has been able to work his schedule to assist at home a great deal… thus freeing me up at times. Also, he benefits from a close relationship with the children.

A typical quote from an employed mother:

My husband has always been very supportive of my work status. While neither of us has had to travel too much, I work long hours, and often bring work home. He does all of the cooking, and most of the food shopping (otherwise we split pretty "conventionally" along gender lines)!

Of the 30 percent who commented that their spouses were "ok" with their chosen work status, 46 percent were originally at home in 1994 compared to only 15 percent who were employed in 1994. Why do so many mothers who were at home in 1994 feel their husbands are "ok" in their support? Are the at-home mothers—those who have a passion to be present for their children and who expect to be responsible for most of the chores involved in raising a family—not frustrated by the "traditional" gender roles and thus are happy their husbands supported this in the early years? And then, are these mothers happy that their husbands support a wish to change their work status?

The two higher percentages of employed mothers are split between the categories separated/not thrilled (36%) and we work together (32%). Are the employed mothers who are trying to alter the "traditional gender roles" feeling their spouses are in the category not thrilled with their work status because they do not step in to care for children and home? And are the mothers who wrote they work together happy with the amount their husbands do step in because their husbands are sharing all responsibilities to assure that children and home are happy, healthy and functioning?

I think part of the reason for the discrepancy in the responses of the employed mothers is related to how smoothly the couples had figured out who was responsible for what and when regarding the care of their children. Those who had figured it out claim they "work together." The mothers who wrote their spouses were "not thrilled" were struggling.

The other support question asked was "is your spouse supportive of your work status in general or during a particular time? Please comment." Although the question is similar to the one asking how the spouse demonstrated support, this one about the existence of support generated categories on the ways in which the mothers felt supported—or not.

By far, most (52%) of the mothers whose spouses "respected contribution" were at home in 2008. That year, 26 percent of the employed mothers cited their spouse had "respect for contribution" and 26 percent were "fine *but.*" (*See* Appendix, Graph 18.)

The mothers' comments in the category "respect for contribution," reveal that spouses appreciated different types of contributions made by at-home mothers from those made by employed mothers. The at-home mother's statement below conveys the gist of the type of contribution that is along traditional gender lines, caring for the children and the home:

> I think he has liked my availability to him, for his needs, and he has stated that "he could never do what [name] does, with respect to the kids," and he is appreciative that I have been there for them.

Whereas this quote from an employed mother's description of her husband's support is about respect for her work and her financial contribution:

> My husband has always been 100% supportive of my work. He has arranged his schedule to accommodate mine, we plan business trips together, and he likes the fact that I am financially independent.

The second category, with 26 percent of employed mothers was: "fine *but*"—meaning, like the "divorced/not thrilled" category that emerged in their response regarding *if* they were supportive—their husband's demonstration of support was not great. Perhaps they could show their support by helping more around the home, or with the children, or recognizing the importance of her employment? In short, they could use improvement. This employed mother's observation exemplifies the "fine *but*" feelings:

He's always been supportive but at the same time, would prefer me to take time off when a child was sick as opposed to him.

Although only a small percentage (22%) of all the mothers in the study (26% of employed and 10% of the at-home mothers in 2008) expressed frustration with the lack of full support from their husbands, there is a pervasive theme to their dissatisfaction. Going back to the experience of the doctor and her husband, the societal myth that children and home are our—we mothers'—responsibility can be seen. Some of us continue with the instilled societal myth as evidenced by this employed mother's statement:

There was a time when I wanted him to notice how overwhelmed I was and pitch in. That never happened. I have, however, learned to recognize that I can't expect him to take on my priorities as his own. I have cut back on professional responsibilities in order to do more things at home.

Like many of us, originally the doctor and the mother quoted above, would have liked more help from their husbands, but did not ask for it. Why? Have we bought society's expectations of the 1950s that it is our duty to care for home and hearth? Why do some of us not ask for help? Why do we adjust our schedules to assure we are completing what "society" decreed we do?

Why do our husbands not "step in" and notice how "overwhelmed" we are? Do they see children and home as our bailiwick also? Let us turn the tables, keeping the values of the 50s—are they solely responsible for the financial stability and lifestyle of the family? Do women/mothers have no obligation in this area?

If we no longer want to live with the gender roles as defined in the 1950s, then who but us will live differently? How will we do that? While our husbands may have their magical moments, they are not mind readers. If we want their involvement, we have to ask!

Further, if we are so lucky as to have a spouse ask if we want a hand, we can learn as the doctor did, to say, "yes." And add to that a "please" and "thank you". People—and our husbands are definitely people—like to be recognized, respected, and appreciated. We certainly do, too! Then hard as it is, we have to try not to correct what he has done!! That is a huge mistake many of us make and I know I am guilty of opening my critical mouth. If your spouse is anything like my husband, he will say or think "my efforts are wrong so I will not bother to try." We need to be appreciative and supportive of his efforts, and keep our sense of humor. In a recent text message I received from my daughter, she said that she sent her boyfriend—now her fiancé—grocery shopping for her and then bemusedly observed, "Considering the versions of things he bought it's as if he were telling me to never send him grocery shopping again!"

A lot of what we think is important, really is not. Maybe this conclusion is just like the mother who said she "learned to recognize that I can't expect him to take on my priorities as his own." The question becomes: "Is what I think needs to be done, really important? And if so, can I let go and appreciate that there are different ways of doing something? Is it possible my way isn't the only way and, of course, the right way?" Hint: if we want their help, then it is best we acknowledge and appreciate their creative ways.

According to the cultural anthropologist, Margaret Mead, "Nobody has ever before asked the nuclear family to live all by itself in a box the way we do. With no relatives, no support, we've put it [the nuclear family] in an impossible situation." The result is that often parents and family members from our childhood—our family of origin—are not around. And thus, we have to work harder to get the support that we need from parents and siblings. Sometimes we may have to reach out. If we feel our parents are supporters of our efforts with our family, work status, and home, and they do not live near us, then we have to call, text, Skype/FaceTime to keep in touch and let them know what is going on in our lives and where and when we might need support. The support might be physical—"come stay with the grandchildren, I need your help"—or, emotional—"I'm making a change and I'm not sure it's the right one."

Given that we like to feel supported and we want approval for our efforts; in addition to asking about spousal support, I asked the mothers if they felt they received support for their work status from their parents and siblings, children, and friends.

The chart below, which is derived from the responses of all the mothers in the study, shows the percentage of mothers in each of the categories regarding the type of support they felt they received from their parents and/or siblings.

Type of Support from Family

Very proud/what doing	51%
Uninvolved	14%
Covert judgment	25%
Doesn't apply/parents diseased	10%
Total	100%

Similarly, a comparison of the work status groups in 2008 was the same. Approximately half of both work status groups felt their parents were very proud of what they were doing. About a quarter of the mothers thought their parents or siblings secretly did not really approve of their work status—were holding covert judgment—and the rest (14%) noted that their parents were uninvolved. It seems that no matter how old we get, parental approval is desirable. That is not to say that we will do as we think they would wish, but we are always happier to have our choices and behaviors confirmed. (Parents are powerful—mothers are parents.)

Another dynamic that affects family support is sibling rivalry. Some of us are mature and support our siblings no matter what and are proud of their achievements. Others of us retain that competitive streak and if we feel we are undeservedly "neglected or criticized" by our parents, then the sibling may get the "blame." What is the difference— why do some appreciate and others feel threatened? Self-confidence obviously plays a role, but what if we feel there is favoritism? (Which, of course, we would not like, unless we were the favorite.) Would we take it out on our "favored" sibling by criticizing what s/he does or what support s/he received from our parents?

A friend of mine related that when she was starting to study for her doctorate, her sister said to her, "Dad is wondering why you are doing this; he doesn't think you will ever finish." Ouch! No support from her father! But what about her sister? Did she really need to tell her this? Sibling rivalry, perhaps?

The following quote from a mother who was at home in 1994 but later changed her work status to part time, demonstrates the subtlety of sibling rivalry and subsequent feelings of parental disapproval:

> My mother immediately asked what would happen to the children with me working even though my sister works full time outside the home. She and my father have helped her enormously over the years driving the kids here or there, picking them up from choir practice etc. She also asked this even though she knew my husband was home almost full time at the start.

Most of the comments were brief and went from outright support: yes, very supportive, to a mixed message from the parental front: My mother told me she envied me, my father thinks women belong at home to lack of support: No, they all thought I worked too much.

Sometimes the "support" comes across in terms of expectations rather than an evaluation of work status choice. I can remember going off to college in the 1960s and being told by my mother that she would be surprised if I did not get married while in college. Nothing was said about the type of studying or work I might be able to do. I did not feel any support for professional pursuits and the curious part to me is I did not notice the lack of this support! I did not think about doing anything but teaching. No one said to me I could be a doctor, lawyer, or architect and I never had the thought. In response to any question about what I wanted to do, I said, "teach math in junior or senior high school." No one commented one way or another.

My observation of the few friends who were not going to be teachers or nurses—but were going to be lawyers—is that they all had fathers who had said to them, "you go girl, you can do anything." As I said, parents are influential. But what is stopping us from reaching beyond their judgments and values and establishing our own? Given the obvious support or independent thought many of the mothers in my study felt, woman have made progress in handling the expectations of parents and plans for themselves about what they can do in the workforce and at home.

A comparison of the types of support employed and at-home mothers received from friends reveals an interesting difference. While both groups had high percentages in both categories, slightly more than half of the at-home mothers in 2008 were in the category "same work status"—their friends from whom they gained support were also at home. Whereas, the highest percentage, which was just slightly less than half of the employed mothers in 2008, were in the category "worked together/respectful of what each other did." (*See* Appendix, Graph 19.)

Why would one group mostly choose a passive description—"same status" and the other group predominantly choose the active words "work together?" Do employed mothers more frequently feel they are "on the run" and thus, need friends who are also in motion? Several comments indicated that their friends were people with whom they worked. Is that because they can save time in arranging social gatherings? Or, your workplace friend will be supportive if you have to cancel because a project is due? Do at-home mothers seek each other out by finding people who are "outside" the workforce—outside the mainstream of activity? Does a friendship begin among at-home mothers because they are searching for someone similar—someone of the same status?

When I was an at-home mother with young babies, I went to several activities: Gymboree, baby swimming, children's play groups, all with the purpose of finding other mothers and potential friends. The activities—as inspiring as they were—were not what drew my attention. For at-home mothers, is the "work status"—the availability of other mothers, the primary drawing card for friendship rather than the activity that brings them together?

In response to my question about what support they felt they received from their children, there is a suggestion of an underlying influence of the traditional gender role expectations. In short, society says "good mothers" are at-home. In 2008, more than half of the at-home mothers (59%) wrote that their children "accepted" their work status. Translation: the children see their mother as doing what mothers are expected to do—take care of children. No big deal, nothing exciting, just what is expected. However, the percentage of employed mothers was higher than at-home mothers on three other types of support they received from their children. The first (21%) was in the category labeled "totally/proud." These mothers proudly reiterated the respectful and inquiring support they received from their children who were eager to learn about them and their employment. Only 4 percent of at-home mothers noted their children were "very proud" of their mother's work status.

A few quotes below from proud employed mothers:

> My children were accustomed to my working and they often accompanied me to work, where they helped out and developed friendships with my colleagues. They took pride in my work, too.

> Both daughters have always expressed their support of my work (partly because they have always known me as a career woman since they were born). They seemed proud to talk about their mother as a female executive… I often shared stories about my work and taught them life lessons from my work/travel experiences.

A second percentage—14 percent employed and no at-home mothers—identified a category "liked/wanted me home." And the third percentage—14 percent employed and 9 percent at-home mothers—were in the category marked "not happy."

Do you think it is possible the children of employed mothers are playing into their mother's vulnerability to feel guilty about "not always being available?" (*See* Appendix, Graph 20.) If all children know is what they have experienced, where do they get the idea their mother is not home enough? Visiting friends whose mothers are at home would be one source for sure, but where else? Being aware of lack of grandparental support? Daddy being annoyed that mommy is not home yet? Or, is it from children whose mothers were at home in 1994 but then sought employment when the children were in elementary school (56%) or junior high school (20%)? Or, are children just being children and focused on themselves?

The quote below from an employed mother has a suggestion of guilt:

> My children are generally supportive, although they like it best when I am home (e.g. not working and at their beck and call)

As does this quote at the thought of employment, from a mother who was always at home:

> They all wanted me home. My youngest son told me he could play board games if I was bored when I mentioned the thought of working part time when he was in middle school. He also said it wouldn't be the same if I wasn't home. How do you argue with that?

At one time or another we all talk about or think about needing support, getting support, and giving support. Can we safely assume that personal support for who we are and what we do is important to our sense of well-being? These mothers articulated areas they received support from their husbands, other family members, and friends. Support from our husbands is complex and continuous. We each can fall into expectations or behaviors reminiscent of traditional gender roles. We do best if we are aware of this and feel the freedom to mention or question our assumptions. Friendships seem to be critical to our survival…who else knows what it is like to be a mother? Who knows better than another mother?

As we have learned from the many different responses from all mothers, people are different. Some people who are introverts or loners do not naturally or easily seek friendship from cohorts or other family members. Do they really not want others around or, do they not know how to get the support—the confirmation—that they are cared about as people and great as they are? Support from family members, friends and cohorts at the workplace or in community organizations show their caring—or not, in different ways. And, individuals may or may not want support from different people depending upon the situation as they see it. But, bottom line, can we assume that support to our being is important and valuable to our sense of self and energy to pursue our interests and care for our family? If we need or want support, we can always ask for it—after all, aren't we worth it?

Chapter 10

Are The Gloves Off Yet?

Who wants to fight? Not mothers. Most of us claim with a certainty that if we were in charge of the world there would be much fewer wars. While the "fight" between at-home and employed mothers is hardly a "world war" or even a "fight," the social mantras of criticism about mothers in either work status is unsettling. What do we assume about a mother if we learn she is one work status or the other?

First, unlike many of the other topics we have discussed, the negative commentary focuses on mothers who have chosen their work status. No criticism is addressed to the single mother who works to support her family. Nor is criticism directed at an at-home mother if the reason for her work status is valued by society, such as having a sick or challenged child; personal illness; education for employment; or problems with affordable daycare. The mothers who have a choice are the ones that conjure up the rebuke from others.

We—members of our society—assume that employed mothers are frequently stressed, rush from one demand to another, and scramble to be available to their children, but are often absent from school or sports events. And we readily assume that at-home mothers are not very interesting or particularly bright and tend to be boring. According to the Pew Research Center, U.S. Bureau of Labor,

(*Harvard Business Review*, public opinion 9-11-2012) only 12 percent thought mothers should work—be employed—full time! Regarding part-time "work" 40 percent were in favor and 42 percent thought a mother should not "work" at all—supporting the traditional value that a woman's place is at home with the children. These 2012 public opinions are what drive the friction between employed and at-home mothers—it is not a personal value, it is a social value. For employed mothers, society's mantra is that mothers belong at home with their children and if you are not at home, then you are not a good mother. For at-home mothers, society's mantra is that you are a mother, not a professional, not a person in your own right—thus, not very interesting or particularly smart.

Mothers who are employed by choice, and those who are at home by choice, periodically feel defensive about their choices.

Recently I was talking with a doctor friend—double checking if indeed these critical social attitudes still have an effect—she said that she and sometimes pregnant doctors receive disapproval about their plans to continue practicing medicine because they are or will be mothers. Were these voices of older mothers who were projecting their own values? Were these voices of contemporaries who were staying home? I do not know, but these rebukes could stem from the traditional social opinion. Why would anyone criticize a woman who has worked hard to achieve her employment status and has a passion to continue? Would we criticize her if she were not also a mother? Yes, if we believe that women should not have paid employment of any kind. And, I trust, some of us do have that opinion—is it cultural? Or, is it the voice of men? Why do we insist on challenging the decision of another? Do we feel threatened by her choice? Are we unsure of our own? Or, are we preempting "the critical voice" of society?

An at-home mother said that she felt like a non-person at social functions. When men or women learned that she was a stay-at-home mother, although they did not turn their backs—which had been my experience—they asked questions only about her children. They did not inquire about her interests or possible previous employment.

Very proudly she told me that she used to travel around the world as a consultant—she had a very important and high-powered job! I trust the people with whom she was talking at a social function thought they were being polite and involving, but this mother felt belittled and personally disregarded. Are we again seeing the result of society's attitude playing out in this interaction? Did the people assume this mother was "just a mother" and thus, had nothing else about which to converse?

A friend of mine used to talk about the interplay between her—an at-home mother—and her very good friend/neighbor—a full-time employed mother. When her children were young, she was at home but her neighbor was not. The neighbor worked very hard with her husband in his business. Not once, but on several occasions, my friend would be at home and the doorbell would ring. One of the neighbor's children would be at her door—locked out of the house and not having any place to go. My friend loved the children and they were always welcome. She was, however, annoyed. *Not* because her neighbor was employed full time. But rather, her neightbor did not acknowledge my friend's efforts to help her out and step in to care for her children. Is lack of appreciation for the efforts of the other—the mother in a different work status—one factor that perpetuates an underlying irritation? Perhaps.

I asked the mothers what their perceptions were of mothers in the "other work status." when their children were young. Four categories emerged from their comments about mothers in the "other" work status: respect, jealous, critical, and questions choice—meaning to question one's own work status choice.

The employed mothers do not strongly group in any particular category—ranging from 31 percent writing about "respect," to 27 percent having a comment that "questions choice," to 21 percent in the category "jealous," to 20 percent being "critical." On the other hand, the at-home mothers in 1994 have two prominent categories that emerge: 38 percent expressing respect for employed mothers and 37 percent expressing criticism of employed mothers. The mothers who were at home in 1994 seem to have distinct and dichotomous feelings about employed mothers when their children were young. (*See* Appendix, Graph 21.)

A few quotes from mothers who were at home in 1994 describe these feelings. First, those demonstrating respect:

> I have always admired women who have sought out a career. The degree of organization that is required to successfully tend to a family and a career simultaneously is tremendous. I do not have that energy.

> I think I was often envious of women who seemed to be able to balance a career with motherhood—and still

end up with good kids. However, I do not think my issues were really about the balance—I think my work issues exist by themselves—I was conflicted about career before I was married, and before I was a mother. These issues have to do with my own feelings about competence, identity, etc. I was raised between the 50's model (Leave it to Beaver) and Gloria Steinem—by the time she came along I was 17, and my belief system was already in place. I did not grow up "frustrated" that women couldn't do certain things, so I did not feel suddenly "free" to realize my childhood dreams.

In addition to these quotes, most within the "respect" category were nonjudgmental comments: "Every mother has to make her own choice," or "it's a personal decision," and:

I was uneasy in my choice so I understand myself in relation to them. I now realize that it is challenging no matter the path and the best choice is to support each other.

Now, that would be really nice if we could all do that!

These comments from mothers at home in 1994 were in the "critical" category—the emotion is tangible:

I felt the mothers who worked outside the home were there because they either didn't like being a full-time care-giver or the couple wanted more income. I thought their values were materialistic, and yes, selfish.

I was a bit sensitive to "working" mothers' comments about how rough they had it and how it must be nice to have so much free time! I also did not like how some of these moms would try to take advantage by "dumping" their kids on me. I got better as time went on about making my expectations clear.

I have worked in the community with some women who work full time plus even though they have babies and they are perfectly able financially to stay home if they want. I did find that difficult to understand particularly when I heard so much from them about how stressful it is and what with the day nanny, the night nanny and the weekend nanny—I had to ask myself if I was being selfish to think why did they want the kids in the first place if they do not actually spend much time with them.

Comments from employed mothers in 1994 are equally strong, reflecting society's unfavorable opinion that mothers at home are not very bright or interesting:

> I still do not know how full-time moms do it, though. I would go batty, and I frankly believe that most stay-at-home moms are pretty limited intellectually.

> I came to the realization that staying home would be rewarding and boring ... I also felt that their lives are very limited to their children and their homes. They're missing out on so much that are going on in the world. Their conversations and interests are also limited. Once their children become more independent, many realized they do not have much to speak of outside of their household accomplishments. Most are totally dependent financially on their husbands—not an ideal situation...

In the quote below, an employed mother chastises other employed mothers who choose to work long hours that limit their availability to their children. Availability was a crucial issue to employed mothers and a cause of stress. While all mothers cite availability as very important to them, the social mantra for employed mothers often includes the idea that employed mothers are not available to their children:

> I probably harbor some negative feeling about mothers who worked long hours, especially if it wasn't financially necessary, and if the children were latch keyed or left with babysitters too often.

What is interesting is the difference between the percentages of employed and at-home mothers who cited feelings of jealousy about mothers of the "other" work status. Only 6 percent of at-home mothers write about feeling jealous but a full 21 percent of employed mothers mention feelings of jealousy. What are they jealous of?

This at-home mother's comment articulates the common theme of jealousy—employed/career mothers have a professional passion that at-home mothers either do not have or have put on hold to care for her children:

> I do not think I envied the women who just "worked," but rather the ones who had "big jobs" or "careers" and seemed to have a drive and an attachment to the work. I am still trying to figure out "what I want to do when I grow up."

And this at-home mother feels jealous of the "other's" apparent success in career and motherhood. She also brushes off—saying it does not apply to her—society's stigma at-home mothers are focused on home and hearth and are not interesting.

> I deeply envied women who had demanding jobs and still had great kids and great connections with those kids. I also didn't have a lot in common with women who stayed home. I am maternal, but not domestic.

These comments below from employed mothers articulate the basis for their jealousy. Not surprisingly, it is their belief that the at-home mothers are not pulled in many directions and thus, have time for their children and themselves.

> I envied them somewhat because they didn't have the constant hassles with juggling work with parenting—like when the kids got sick, or during summer vacation, or when day care arrangements fell thru or didn't seem ideal. I had taken a year off when my daughter was born and I thoroughly enjoyed my time with the other at-home moms in my neighborhood. I reluctantly went back to work for financial reasons. I enjoyed my job very much, but I hated the constant stress of trying to equally allocate time to being a mom and to advancing my career.

> In 1994 I think I had mixed feelings about women who stayed at home with their children—I usually felt a little sorry for them (thinking they must be bored and miss adult conversations) but also felt a little envious that they had more time to be with their children. Now, I still have mixed feelings, but more of the envious kind than the sympathy kind.

> I was envious of mothers who stayed home with their children. Well, they didn't stay home as much as drove the children around, went to the health club, were at school for volunteer meetings, played bridge, and joined book clubs that met during the day. It was

probably also a financial envy—these were mothers who didn't have to work and still had a lot of household help.

And then a thoughtful, not-so-positive observation from an employed mother:

> I was worried in 1994 that I was making a mistake (being a bad mother). I am more confident now that this was the right path for me and my family. I must admit, I see a lot of women who have not worked become lost in their 40s and beyond. As the kids age, they get sidetracked by shopping, yoga etc. Over time, some of these women have become less confident, self-indulgent, etc. I think it's a sad waste of talent.

Although I do not believe the above results or comments would change significantly, keep in mind that because I asked the mothers in 2008 about their experiences in social situations fourteen years earlier—in 1994—their responses, based on memory, could be different from their feelings in 1994. Our memories are very complicated. How we remember an event is composed of our perception of an event when we are experiencing it, a history of our experiences and reactions to similar events, and our belief systems. You can see suggestions of change in their feelings toward mothers of the other work status in some of their comments already cited. Did this affect their retelling of their perceptions in 1994? Does it matter if it does? Only so we do not take anything as fact but rather as an observation worth noting.

You might assume that a perception you have about another group would embody reactions you had to that group when in social situations—this would be an example of "history of our experiences and reactions," but evidently not. The perceptions of mothers in the "other" work status did not always correspond with how mothers felt when asked about their experiences in social situations.

For example, one mother's perception was: "I think I've always had respect for moms who chose different options…" and in her reaction to social situations she described: "As a stay-at-home mom, I found it difficult to make casual conversation with people at parties. Working people seem to have little interest in talking to a stay-at-home mother."

Another mother's perception was: " I did not judge other people…" and her reaction to social situations she described: "I felt uncomfortable a few times at my husband's company functions…some of the spouses were working full time—they were not interested in talking to me."

Both of these mothers and many others are able to separate their own experiences from a general perception they hold about a group. Given this, what does influence their perception? Is it based in self-confidence about their own choice? Is it an intellectual perception that rejects society's mantra about the "other" work status group and not a personal observation and not based on personal experiences?

Most of the mothers who were at home in 1994 (60%) wrote that they felt rejected or found themselves questioning their work status choice in social situations when their children were young. Comments from originally at-home mothers:

> I did feel awkward in social situations as a result of not having a job to refer to or to give me "status," but I do not believe it was anything that other people did or said to me, but rather me trying to find/define who I now was in the world.

> I was a senior lawyer [in the government] when I [started my family] and quit working. At dinner parties involving my husband's law firm... it was painfully amusing how many times people moved on as soon as they realized I was "just" a stay at home mom. This was true even with people who had known me as a lawyer, even one guy I had actually supervised. Once I had no title, I was nothing to him.

Once again societal expectations play a role in the treatment of at-home mothers in social situations:

> Oh, a great conversation stopper at gatherings was the reply to the question usually placed by a male "And what do you do?" I mean, any woman who stays at home to raise her children must be pretty uninteresting and of no consequence for networking purposes! I found that if I went to a social gathering without my

husband (usually travelling) very few bothered to engage me in conversation.

In contrast, most of the mothers who were employed in 1994 did not fall into any particular category; the highest percentage (27%) was also in a category that was imbued with rejection. Descriptions of their experiences are captured in these few quotes below:

> I was always a full-time worker but on those rare days I took vacation to just do regular things, I would meet stay-at-home moms at the park. Their friendship, frankly, would "stop" when they found out I was a working mom—I guess they were anxious for friends during business hours!

> I was usually shunned by non-working mothers; my children were not encouraged to play with their children. Not all the time but often enough that we all felt the sting.

> When the kids were younger and I was working crazy hours, whenever we were with friends I talked about my kids all the time just as much as the other mothers. I tried to avoid talking about my job, but I'm sure I did to some degree. We never seemed to get as many invitations as the others in our social groups… I think it's a combination of the other mothers feeling a bit intimidated by me or not as smart as me or something

along those lines. Again, this is almost completely a group of stay-at-home moms. I've never felt that stay-at-home moms should be out working, but maybe some of the mothers in our group felt inadequate around me—or maybe just the opposite—maybe they thought it was terrible that I spent so little time with my kids.

You might have noticed that at-home mothers reference social situations that suggest parties or special-occasion gatherings when assessing their reactions. In contrast, employed mothers reference general encounters with mothers who are at-home when assessing their reactions to others when they learn about their work status. This different focus makes sense given what one of the at-home mothers cited in her quote above: special occasions are opportunities to network—employed mothers can and do consciously network; typically at-home mothers do not.

I wondered about the reaction of employed mothers who were teachers—particularly preschool teachers. My thinking was they really would not be "useful" for business networking purposes. One mother summed up her reaction: "Pre-school teacher and community volunteer: not very flashy or sexy. I usually end[ed] up talking about my last full-time employment..." However, feeling left out or not included in networking—not always business related—is not exclusive to at-home mothers. One employed mother wrote: "I did... feel that the stay-at-home mothers seemed to have more of a network established—they were able to get together during the day more often with each other" or, "the [at-home] moms would get together without the husbands, so they developed stronger friendships, and I wasn't part of that." No one likes to feel left out and if we notice that there is a group in which we are not included, a small part of us feels left out even if we claim we do not want to be part of that group. We all have feelings.

The second highest grouping for employed mothers (20%), developed the category "everyone the same." Their comments reflect their tendency to be around other employed mothers, which I discussed briefly in Chapter 9: Who Gives Us Support?

Because employed mothers have very little time for friends on an everyday basis, most of their friendships come from the office. Consequently, it is no surprise that their social situations comprise other employed mothers. Typical comments were: "It was never a problem because most of the other men had wives in the same situation" and, "Most other mothers worked also, so I never felt awkward."

Do these feelings of rejection and criticism change—ameliorate—over time? Do mothers whose children are launched either to college or the world beyond high school, feel they receive different reactions to their work status when in social situations? What are the effects of experience, time, and maturity on the reception they get in social interactions about their work status?

I asked if the social reaction changed, as their children got older. Only 27 percent of all the mothers checked "yes." Most of their comments reflected the passage of time. A little less than half of the mothers (41%) felt that others "accepted" them—most everyone was in the same work status. And, slightly more than half of the mothers (54%) were split between (28%) "expected"—employment was okay now that their children were older, and (26%) "criticized" (26%) for their work status choice.

The categories that emerged from the comments of employed and at-home mothers convey a wonderful picture of change in reaction to social situations when the at-home mothers became employed. Why this change? Is one reason for a new reaction because society's opinion, "a mother belongs in the home," no longer has the same impact when the children are launched or at minimum, no longer babies? Or, is society's critical attitude about employed mothers really, "a mother of babies and toddlers belongs at home but it is okay to find employment when children are older?"

Psychology studies typically state that the first two years of a child's life are critical to his or her development. Many of the mothers who were at-home and changed to employment when their children were in elementary school wrote that they "felt it was important to be home for the child's early years" and they are very glad that they were. Perhaps the psychology research provides a theoretical basis for a seeming shift in the social mantra.

Not one at-home mother in 2008 wrote that the reaction they received in social situations about their work status was "ok/expect." This is because they were not doing what was expected now that the children were older. They were expected not to remain at home. To support this social reaction is the fact that half of the at-home mothers were in the category "criticized." It seems that society is changing its mantra for at-home mothers too: if a mother no longer has very young children she belongs in the workforce! (*See* Appendix, Graph 22.)

A few quotes from some of these at-home mothers support this concept:

If anything, especially after my husband died, I feel that the "she's just being lazy" attitude has become stronger from casual acquaintances. I hear "When are you going back to work?" from a lot of casual acquaintances. I get the sense that they think great big teenagers can look after themselves and I'm just spoiling them by driving them to school, supervising homework, making home cooked meals, etc. The dangers of 16-year-old drivers, unsupervised teens (especially in this area), and benefits of family dinners, etc., do not seem to register nor the continued emotional fallout from their father's death.

As my children got older, there were more questions as to whether I was going to return to the workplace, or take up some pursuit to "do something with all my free time."

Employed mothers, however, do not get a waiver from society's negative assessment. They still feel criticized for not being available to their children:

There seems to be an expectation in the world of children's sports that parents be very involved and attend all events (this is at the jr. high and high school level—and the travel teams). I had to have a conversation with both daughters to say "If I do not come to your games it doesn't mean I do not love you" and have gotten some strange looks from other parents when I tell them I do not attend all events.

Mothers all felt judged interacting with teachers, principals, or other parents when in their children's school—not just social situations. Their memories of when their children were young and they were involved in the school or with fundraising activities are as expected. The mothers who aided the teachers were primarily the mothers who were available—the at-home mothers. Looking at the responses from their 2008 work status, you can see that reflecting back to when their children were young, the at-home mothers (60%) felt appreciated compared to a much smaller percent of the employed mothers (29%). Slightly more of the employed mothers (37%) than the at-home mothers (30%) felt no problem—not positive or negative. And only the employed mothers felt "negative reactions from other parents." (*See* Appendix, Graph 23.)

An interesting observation from an employed mother who noted the assumption by which everyone operated—at-home mothers are the ones who are more readily available:

> There was an unspoken expectation that at-home moms would step up first when volunteers were needed at school even if they had major volunteer responsibilities outside of school, e.g. political, religious, other community organizations.

This employed mother's comment did not fall into either the "appreciated" or "no problem/fair" categories. Her quote below is representative of those who felt frustrated with the school because the teachers were seemingly not accommodating their efforts to be involved. Her frustration is palpable:

> You would think that teachers (most of whom were, after all, working parents) would understand, but they didn't. I was also irritated when teachers would assign a project during the week that required parents to buy something that night. I asked them to make those assignments earlier, so that we had a weekend to do the purchasing, but, again, that fell on deaf ears.

Because people and situations are not all the same or perceived the same by everyone, the employed mother's statement below embodies the opposite from the above mother's frustrations. This employed mother felt her work status was recognized and respected. She had no negative experience—her comment is typical of those in the "treated fair" category:

> As for teachers and principals, there never were any negative comments about my working instead of being at home. Teachers, in particular, understand the balancing act of parenting and job.

Most of the at-home mothers' comments about the appreciation they felt from their school experiences were similar to these quotes below:

> I think the teachers have generally been extremely happy and grateful to all the stay-at-home moms since we did most of the volunteering and always showed up for things on time.

> I found the teachers and the principal welcoming to stay at home moms. Sometimes the working parents felt conflicts because they couldn't do the same things as stay at home moms.

This at-home mother's comment suggests that lack of appreciation may be one reason for the underlying friction between mothers of different work statuses:

> The teachers always were very happy to have stay-at-home mothers since they were the ones to volunteer the most. Most of the parents that were volunteering were stay-at-home parents … and the experiences with them were always positive. When I would call to get help for a school fundraiser or for a class event, there were some full-time working parents that acted like their time was more important and couldn't be bothered. On the other hand, there were more who were unable to help because of their work schedule

but still appreciative of those who were volunteering to help their child's class.

As their children went from elementary school to middle and high school, a small percent (12%) of the mothers did sense a change in the welcome mat at school but, basically, they accepted it. The reasons for the shift were different for the two work status groups.

The employed mothers felt greater approval at school for "more mothers were working so it was not as unusual." Perhaps like their experiences in social situations, now that their children were older, others—in this case, teachers—expected and accepted their work status it got "easier as kids aged and excelled."

The at-home mothers noted that they were no longer needed or wanted in the classrooms. This message, however, from an at-home mother exudes her anger and frustration at the "new" attitude toward parental involvement:

> The teachers in middle school made it abundantly clear that they did not want to see any parents in the school, or even hear from us, under any circumstances, except for an evening event like a play where the parents were invited. When I went to a teacher conference in elementary school, teachers encouraged me to keep in touch with any concerns. By middle school, there were no teacher conferences, and if I asked for one they told me my daughter should speak for herself and told me it was

inappropriate for me to express any concern directly to them.

Was the school setting a policy to encourage parents to "let go" and not "hover" over every activity their children did? From what history did the school officials develop such a stance to develop independence in its students? Did they share their philosophy with the parents?

For the most part, the at-home mothers—71 percent in 2008—still felt appreciated for their work at school. This comment below is representative of those from mothers originally at-home:

> They were always appreciative to have involved parents who cared about grades and showed up at sporting events, etc.

Finally, I wanted to know how the mothers felt about reunions with old school friends or with family. Reunions are interesting. Usually people attend school reunions if 1) they have the time; 2) they feel good about themselves; or 3) they do not feel good about themselves but are confident that they will experience support from the group. (The same usually holds for participating in surveys.) This quote addresses the feeling:

> I avoid reunions like the plague. I think I do not want to confront all the others who have "done it all." So, even though I am comfortable with my decision, on some level I guess I am defensive about it.

Depending on family dynamics, people may have a choice to go or not but the pressure is different—expectations can run high. On the other hand, given that many family members are scattered and very busy, organizing a family reunion can be a challenge and may not occur for many.

The memories of the mothers about their experiences with reunions when their children were young are shown in the table below. Two categories—shown bold and italicized—are again dichotomous: 38 percent of the mothers felt their family and friends were proud of their work status, and 25 percent of the mothers felt either criticized by friends or family members or critical of themselves or of mothers in the "other work status."

A comparison of the percentage of employed mothers in these categories with the percentage of at-home mothers reveals little difference between the groups—they are pretty evenly split; the largest difference was at-home mothers reported 3 percent higher in the "critical" category.

Experiences at Reunions by At-Home Mothers	Percent
Everyone same	10
Family/friends proud	**38**
Self-report done well	4
Rejected/criticized or critical of "others"	**25**
Self-confident/indifferent what others think	10
Didn't attend	13
Total	100.0

A few negatives from at-home mothers:
Friends and Co-workers said condescendingly that "they wish they could afford to stay home."

My status generally is home with my children. I usually had to do a lot of explaining. Most people didn't understand how someone who had worked hard to get a professional degree would stay home with kids.

Being a stay-at-home mom seemed to cause some jealousy/resentment with sisters-in-law, college reunions, due to the fact (I believe) that they worked while their children were young and continue to work.

Similar to the reactions to social situations and experiences in the children's schools, the response to whether or not the reactions at reunions changed regarding their work status as their children got older, only 11 percent of all the mothers noted that they felt a change. An interesting change in the percentage of mothers in each category that emerged is that "do not attend" went from 13 percent when their children were young to 44 percent of all mothers now that their children are older.

About half of the employed mothers in 2008 were primarily the group that "did not attend" reunions. Whether or not the employed mothers become busier and have more demands on them when the children are older, it is hard to say, but these comments are typical: "I have had no time to attend reunions"; "Didn't go—too busy working."

Slightly less than half of the at-home mothers in 2008 found that people's reactions to them at reunions were similar to their reactions in other social situations and at their children's schools. But unlike the previous reasons—their children are older and the mothers are "expected to work," these mothers have grown to be comfortable with their work status of not being employed and confidently can say that and be accepted by their friends. (*See* Appendix, Graph 24.) You can hear the confidence in these comments below:

> People would ask what my plans were. They implied that I would probably be going back to work. But I just told them as a family we had decided that was not what we wanted to do.

A formerly at-home mother now employed part time wrote:

I think it was understood more how much work three kids are and that I was given more respect because I was working outside the home, no matter how many hours it was.

All the results charts—and comments from the mothers in my study, demonstrate two factors. One is the power of society's mantras about employed mothers being exhausted and not available to their children, and at-home mothers having lots of free time and being not very bright or interesting. These mantras, according to the Pew Research conducted for the Bureaus of Labor and Statistics 2012, confirm that these concepts are still quite powerful.

The sorry impact is that in social situations, in interactions with children's schools, and at reunions, we frequently feel challenged and on the defensive for our work status choices.

The second factor, and the good news, is that the longer we experience our work status choices and changes, the more confident we become and seemingly are less affected by "what others think." Eleanor Roosevelt gave us some excellent advice: "You wouldn't worry so much about what others think of you if you realized how seldom they do." Life is hard enough, we need to be kind to ourselves, appreciative of others, and disregard mantras that are not supportive of our efforts.

Chapter 11

Where Do We Go From Here?

While I was writing this book mothers would ask me: "What did you learn? Can you tell me what I should do?" The simple answer is "no," I cannot tell you what to do.

But I can: 1) identify attitudes and practices in our society that need adjustment; 2) share some observations and suggestions that might make life a little easier; and 3) bring to your attention events and feelings that affected mothers in my study. Many of these issues currently rest in the back of our heads. I want to bring them to the front—where we purposely pay attention, so that we are aware and better prepared for the challenges of motherhood.

I do have one general conclusion which I have stated many times throughout the book: Every mother assesses her personal situation and her values when she decides about her work status—what is best for her and what is best for her family. The decision is personal. No one has the right to criticize her decision. As the discussions in the previous chapters have shown, we are all different. Our situations are different, our values are different and what we think is best for us, is not necessarily best for another mother.

The thoughtful and diverse responses the mothers in my study shared about their experiences, decisions, and feelings while caring for their children, their marriage, and themselves over a period of 14 years is the foundation of my views. Each of us tries very hard to be the best mother we can be. The preparation we get for the role of mother is: 1) our observations and feelings when growing up in our own home; 2) what we observe while in other homes; and 3) what we read about child rearing practices. But, there is no one correct way for everyone in every situation. There are different parenting styles, which I briefly discussed in Chapter 4—authoritative, authoritarian, indulgent, and neglectful. There are also different practices based on pediatric observations and studies—respond immediately to your baby versus put the baby on your schedule. Or, "spare the rod spoil the child" to "time-outs" to "anticipate and discuss the troublesome behavior."

Just to make life more challenging, over time ideas about what is safest for the baby changes too. When my children were babies we were told to put babies on their stomachs to sleep. Now parents are instructed to put babies on their backs to prevent Sudden Infant Death Syndrome (SIDS). This new behavior has had a dramatic effect on reducing the number of SIDS incidents, but pediatricians must now give exercises to increase neck strength, which has not developed as it did when babies were placed on their stomachs. Bottom line: situations and messages are always changing. Motherhood is hard and challenging. All of us try to do the very best we can. We deserve and need respect and support from each other, our families, friends, employers, and society in general.

Some attitudes in society could use some adjustment. Recall that according to Pew Research Center polling results in 2012, only 12 percent of the people interviewed were in favor of full-time employment for mothers and 42 percent thought mothers should not be employed at all. Given these statistics critical of employed mothers, it is evident that the assumption, "employed mothers belong with their children; if she chooses full-time employment she does not care about her children"—is alive and well. If you re-read any of the comments in Chapter 3 on the frustrations the mothers felt about full-time employment, you will see that the social idea about not caring just is not true. The comments from the full-time employed mothers consistently express their profound frustration trying to be available and care for their children—their deep love and concern for them is evident. However, given that it still prevails, what do you do? Ignore it as best you can. Remember Eleanor Roosevelt's words of wisdom. They might help you to focus on what you are doing—your work status choice—not the social criticism. She said, "You wouldn't worry so much about what others think of you if you realized how seldom they do."

Believe in yourself, know yourself, and accept yourself. Continue with what you are doing. Society will eventually catch up and until then, it is a waste of time and energy to pay attention to anyone or situation that holds the mantra to be "truth."

Employed mothers are not the only target of a social mindset critical of their work status. At-home mothers find themselves confronted with the assumption that they are not very bright or interesting. Apparently the British, too, buy into this negative description. An online article in March 2012[†††] questioning the choice of educated mothers to stay at home, included this comment:

[†††] http://www.dailymail.co.uk/femail/article-2115170/Can-woman-clever-stay-home-mum.html#ixzz2ck7xwJ1L

> Many believe that stay-at-home mums lack ambition. This week, Lord Lawson [a member of parliament in 1992] revealed that Margaret Thatcher [when Prime Minister] was reluctant to give tax breaks to women who didn't work because she thought wives who stayed at home "lacked get-up-and-go and gumption."

Was Prime Minister Thatcher, who obviously was an employed mother, looking down on at-home mothers? Really? Did Thatcher think that because the government was so supportive of parental leave, daycare and ways to maintain employment status that no mother would choose to be at home? Whatever her reasoning, her reluctance to give tax breaks seems to give credence to the idea that at-home mothers do not do much—they are uninteresting—they "lack gumption." Did she believe we just sit around and eat bon bons all day?

Given that no poll I am aware of has asked if people think at-home mothers are intellectually challenged, where does this idea come from? Why does it prevail? I think in part, "women's work" has never really been valued in our society. Our cultural values are still predominantly male: money and power. We women certainly do not mind obtaining either but we did not establish these assets as goals. Our society claims to value family, but our policies do little to support families. Personal character traits: kindness, caring, and concern for others are qualities not on the checklist for success—are not articulated as a value—though they undoubtedly play a part. These qualities of compassion we derive from our families, the nurturing we receive. And who is the nurturer according to our society? Mother—the very person society claims is not "very smart or interesting."

I refer you again to Ann Crittenden's book, *If You've Raised Kids, You Can Manage Anything: Leadership Begins At Home* (2004), in which she identifies management skills of multitasking and focusing, empowering and encouraging growth, working well with others to create positive outcomes for all and within an atmosphere of fair play. All these "skills" are what mothers do; we do not have special training or degrees, we instinctively use these tools every day to help our children learn to cope with challenges, get along with others, and become the best they can be. Using these skills effectively requires some "smarts" and it certainly is interesting.

And, as I mentioned previously, in Ms. Crittenden's first book, *The Price Of Motherhood: Why The Most Important Job in the World Is Still The Least Valued* (2001), she discusses the financial and legal policies and social practices that penalize and undermine at-home mothers. There is an undercurrent to change these policies and practices but they still exist and send a message. Lip service is what at-home mothers get and much of that includes the critical social mantra. We are, I think, still in trouble.

Europeans—those Europeans whose governments have extensive policies for family leave, childcare, and employment conditions—really have a choice to be employed or stay at home with the children. The message seems to be if you have a chance to have someone or someplace to take good care of your children, you can pursue your interests. Perhaps missing is the message that a mother may actually have a passion to stay home and grow her children.

Like the mothers in my study, some European mothers, given a choice, do opt out of the work force to care for their children. But, these at-home mothers receive another form of social criticism. As the current Prime Minister of Denmark, Helle Thorning-Schmidt, said in the above-mentioned online article, "British women are wasting their education by becoming stay-at-home mothers."

Educated British women who did opt out rebuked this comment by first reiterating their passion: "I've always known I wanted to stay at home to bring up my children. No one else can replicate that bond of love." And then, the comment below articulates how this commenter uses her education in the role of at-home mother—defending her choice:

> My knowledge of history and the intellectual discipline I've gained from my education has enriched my children's lives. At Oxford, I learned to think and write cogently, to analyze, discuss, to be self-confident—and I have passed on all these skills to my children. Motherhood is a constant challenge. You use all your practical skills—you paint, read, garden and cook with them; you imbue them with enthusiasm for life. Even when they are just pottering along at your side, they are learning and conversing. Child-rearing dull? Not for one moment.

Although Europe far exceeds the United States in support of families, a critical social mantra—at least regarding at-home mothers—still exists.

Given the differences noted between the support given to families by European countries and the U.S., the U.S. needs to do better, and can. We—mothers—need Congress to pass more supportive family leave practices, provisions for free day care, and protection in the workforce for family leave. A conference titled "The Shriver Report: A Woman's Nation Pushes Back from the Brink,"[‡‡‡] (January, 2014) addressed these very issues. Congressional leaders, renowned researchers, educators and program directors discussed the policies and programs needed to move women—and children—away from the brink of poverty.

Government and private companies could alter some of their unfriendly family policies to enable mothers to continue full-time employment. As Anne-Marie Slaughter explained in her controversial article, "Why Women Still Can't Have it All,"[§§§] she returned to an academic life that provided a relatively fluid schedule over which she had some control. She chose the academic position over the prestigious and all-consuming position of Director of Policy and Planning for the U.S. State Department because "… working long hours on someone else's schedule, I could no longer be both the parent and the professional I wanted to be—at least not with a child experiencing a rocky adolescence."

Corporations and government could provide more opportunities for mothers to work from home or flexi hours. And

---

[‡‡‡] *This conference –*The Shriver Report*– was sponsored by *The Atlantic Monthly* based on a study by Maria Shriver and the Center for American on January 15, 2014, at the Newseum in Washington, D.C.

[§§§] **The Atlantic Monthly* (July/August, 2012),

would it be so difficult for some companies to offer re-training for mothers who were at home but wish to re-enter the workforce? In addition, what about factories? Why not have factories alter their shift schedules to benefit mothers? Why not offer some shifts that do not rotate but are stable so that a mother can have a set schedule to arrange for childcare?

David Shipler in his book, *The Working Poor: Invisible in America* (2005), points out the rigidity of our thinking and the resistance of organizations, agencies, and companies to change. He shares a true story about a single employed mother who takes a job at a factory making more money than she had earned in the past. She had boarders in her home who were available to be there when she worked the late or night shift, so that her 14-year-old daughter was not alone. Unfortunately they moved out and try as she could, she could not find anyone to board. When her daughter's school principal heard her story and anxiety about leaving her daughter alone, he said he would have to call child services because she was being negligent in her care. The school, the mother, and the child welfare agency never thought to contact the factory to ask if the mother could work just the day shift. The entire onus was on the mother, the mother who had minimum resources; the system was not responsive.

Similarly, could other employers that have shifts stop rotations for some of their employees, particularly mothers? Maybe some do, but many do not. Nursing, firefighting, policing are a few occupations that come to mind. Employed mothers have enough upheavals in their lives. They need schedules that are clear and consistent so they can arrange for the care of their children when they are not available.

While we are making progress—albeit slow progress—in changing attitudes and policies to be more supportive of mothers, we can become mindful of some behaviors that we can do to make life easier for us while our children are still at home.

Employed mothers frequently feel and claim that attending to the demands of home and employment is exhausting and frustrating. Given that family is not going away and neither is the workplace, is there anything that you can do to make life easier and calmer for yourself? "No," and "yes." "No," because there is no specific tactic or behavior that I deduced from the comments of the mothers in my study that reveals what to do to solve the frustration from the pulls from family and employment. The "yes" is a reminder to stop wasting energy beating yourself up about not being in two places at once. Being exasperated and anxious does nothing but churn up your stomach and curtail your charming personality. Just be nice to yourself and really feel that you are doing the best you can. Try to be proud of yourself for your good efforts. Share some of these feelings with a good friend—probably another mother. You want to feel validated as a person for all that you are doing. Validation of self is good. Validation of self energizes us. Where do you get validation, and really, how does it make anything better?

Think about it. One of the big differences in conversations with a girlfriend about a problem versus a conversation with your husband about the same problem is that your girlfriend listens, supports, humors, and understands. Phrases such as: "Absolutely!" "I know just how you feel!" "I had the same experience…" frequently permeate such conversations. You feel better, but she has not told you to do anything.

What she has done is relate to you as an intelligent, capable, caring person who is trying very hard to make home, hearth, and employment (or not) productive and positive experiences. Your husband eagerly—unless you have educated him—steps in to tell you what to do to solve the problem. He cares—he really does—and he wants to make things better for you so he has a suggestion. This is *not* what you want. You were not asking him to solve the problem. You were asking him to support you—your feelings—and then, possibly through discussions with him, come up with a course of action. Given that we all do feel better when we receive emotional support and confirmation that we are good, intelligent people, try to share your frustration and concerns with friends and make sure you educate your husband because he can be one of your greatest advocates.

From my study, I do, however, have some practical behavior advice to share with at-home mothers. The most frequent complaints of at-home mothers are: we feel isolated, we miss adult company, and we do not like being financially dependent on our husbands. At-home mothers, because we receive no employee feedback or raises or promotions, as do our counterparts in the workforce, need to be resourceful to obtain this information. We are human and most of us—some more than others— need feedback/validation about ourselves and how well we are doing in each of our roles of mother, daughter, friend, wife, sibling, and volunteer.

If we stay home or go alone to activities with our children and keep to ourselves, we most likely feel lonely. Somehow—however or whatever you do to make yourself feel good and strong as an adult person—do it and do it often. If you are at home caring for your children then you are constantly giving; constantly giving means you are depleting your energy and need to do activities or have conversations that restore you. Try to be creative and think of places or ways you could obtain feedback about yourself that you would value and would make you feel good about yourself.

When I was an at-home mother, I sometimes started a conversation with the person in the checkout line who was in front or behind me in the grocery store. If they had a lot of dog food, I would ask about the dog(s); lots of sodas, I would ask about the party; diapers... Most of the time people were delightful and I enjoyed a brief exchange of similar feelings or experiences. I felt good after these brief exchanges. Sometimes people did not want to talk and I stopped, but most of the time their reaction was very positive; I enjoyed the moment. I chose this behavior because I like people and enjoy connecting and feeling connected—a form of validation for me. Some of our needs are the same—contact and validation—but our ways of obtaining it are different.

Another complaint of at-home mothers is the lack of adult conversation or intellectual stimulation. Given that we are all different, if these forms of communication are important to you, then definitely be resourceful and make sure you get what you need. We always have choices. Try to make what you need a priority for you at least some of the time. Some of the at-home mothers in my study pointedly stated they were not like other at-home mothers. My thoughts about that are: 1) I trust their experiences so far and that is their truth, and 2) if they are at home then there are others like them. Even though I have stressed and continue to support the concept that we are all different and even unique, we are not *that* unique—we are almost never the only one in our situation. This is where you have to be imaginative and seek out or create situations that will provide you the conversation that you feel you need to give you adult, satisfying, stimulating, and even challenging conversation.

The third biggest source of frustration for at-home mothers is the lack of financial independence. This is a real problem for many at-home mothers. Being dependent on your husband's earning, you do not have your own money to spend; to make decisions as you wish; to behave as a financially independent adult being. This situation is, or can be, very demoralizing.

I realize I have offered no practical advice about handling the sensitive topic of finances particularly for at-home mothers, who typically do not have their own source of income. I do not have practical behavioral advice because, as I have written many times, there are a myriad of situations and behaviors that are right for different people at different times. No one way is correct or will work for everyone. My one suggestion is make sure you are clear about your feelings concerning money and money management when you talk with your spouse about how finances will be handled in your new family. Be clear and make sure that you revisit this conversation if and when necessary, which may be more often than you would initially think. A family's financial situation—not the amount but their attitudes and management of their finances—can affect the marriage.

An interesting side point about finances is that society still makes the assumption that the husband is the main resource for all financial issues, despite the fact that mothers with children under 18 are increasingly becoming the "breadwinners" for the family. According to a 2011 Pew poll for the U.S. Census Bureau, in 40 percent of households mothers are the primary or sole source of income.****

We are making progress but still many companies and organizations behave in a very chauvinistic manner. I was the one who established the insurance for our home and cars. I was the contact and I was the reference for payment. Did not matter. When I called to ask a question about our account they had never heard of me. My husband's name—different from mine—was the primary name on the account! Who asked them to do that? It was their policy! Sometimes that phrase drives me nuts. *Change the policy!*

The above suggestion—to know how you feel and what you expect about the handling of money in your family before starting a conversation with your spouse—may not be a startling revelation. But, it does bring attention to the importance of the impact familial financial management has on many mothers. Think about it; pay attention to this issue so that perhaps you can avoid or better handle financial issues and not have some of the negative feelings a few of the mothers in my study experienced.

This intent—to bring attention to issues that may be obvious but assumed rather than purposefully addressed—is the third and final type of information I wish to share. This information too I derived from the responses and comments of the mothers in my study. And, please note, I have no assumption that any of it will bring about an epiphany. What I hope is that the analysis and organization I have given to the thoughtful responses and comments from the mothers will give you advanced notice of issues that you may encounter.

**** Most of these mothers—63% of them—are single mothers but 37% are married.

You can think about some of these issues—move them from the back of your head to the front where you think about what you want, how you feel and what choices you might have or want to have in addressing events that affect you and your family. You will not be blindsided and you will feel more in control.

The first and perhaps the strongest issue is to be aware that we are always, always making choices. Even though there are times when we do not feel we have a choice, we do. What is my point? I want all of us to realize that we do have power. No, I am not suggesting that we march up to a supervisor or potential employer and tell her just what we think. What I am suggesting is that each of us is in charge of our life. In fact, we are the only person or thing over which we do have control. If we are aware of this control, use it to our advantage. Be resourceful, take good care of ourselves. Then we will feel good, and we will have energy to give to each member of our family, and whatever else is important to us.

In addition to paying attention to our choices, we need to examine our situations and values, which we assess when making decisions about our work status and our family. We need to notice—really notice—what is a priority; notice what is important to us. If we pay attention and have time to think and examine our circumstances and feelings, then we can make better decisions for ourselves, and better decisions that affect others.

According to the employed mothers there are several types of challenges that create stress. The first and most prevalent is the ongoing challenge to manage the demands of home and office, which we have already discussed. The second type of challenge is employment situations that create stress: 1) the unwritten but expected long hours at the office; 2) the lack of flexi-time; 3) the absence of the option to telecommute; or 4) the avoidance or penalties related to motherhood— being placed on the "mommy track" at pay reduction. The third type of challenge that creates stress is interpersonal relationships in the office such as problems with supervisor, co-workers, change in management or direction of the company, unexpected change in job description, loss of job, or disappointing promotion. These are potential events employees often encounter; it is the nature of employment. How we respond to these various challenges, whether or not we take charge of ourselves as we find solutions to whatever is causing stress will affect how we proceed in the workforce and how we feel about ourselves as employees and grown adults. We all encounter surprises and disappointments. What makes each of us different from the other is how we handle these events. Do we take control of ourselves and as clearly as possible make decisions that will benefit us and have a positive effect on our future? Or, do we choose to let ourselves feel so angry (rightfully) and defeated that we go along with whatever is offered? Do we have a choice?

Stay-at-home mothers have different stress factors that are related to employment—their attempts to re-enter the workforce. One general difficulty experienced by some mothers was that they did not stay connected with their pre-motherhood employment nor did they keep up their skills/knowledge. If they wanted to go back to the same position they held, they often found that they were behind and could not return to their previous level of employment. Other mothers did not want to go back to their pre-baby employment but found they received no credit for managing family and home.

In addition, both work status groups enumerated personal and familial situations that they learned required a great deal of their time and energy. One not often thought about when we are young is the common situation—if all goes in the expected pattern—we will become the sandwich generation. We will be responsible for our parents—their health, their finances, and lifestyle expectations as they age. Whether they are local or far away, whether they are our parents or our in-laws, whether there are local siblings or other close family members, are all factors that we may have to address and manage. Thinking about practical information such as healthcare, insurance, wills, before we suddenly have to respond to a situation may reduce some of the stress. If we are aware, then we can better prepare and be more in control and make more effective decisions.

The other family, our family with our husband and children—our immediate family—also can produce stress for us. One major and unexpected cause could be the physical, emotional, or academic health of our children, spouse, or ourselves. We cannot plan for this and do not want to be Winnie the Pooh's Eeyore who never sees the bright side of anything:

> Good morning, Pooh Bear," said Eeyore gloomily. "If it is a good morning," he said. "Which I doubt," said he.
>
> "Why, what's the matter?"
>
> "Nothing, Pooh Bear, nothing. We can't all, and some of us do not. That's all there is to it."

"Can't all what?" said Pooh, rubbing his nose.

"Gaiety. Song-and-dance. Here we go round the mulberry bush."

We can be aware that because life is life, it is not always easy. But we can also be aware that there are others who have or have had the same experience; we are not alone. They handled their challenges. We can handle ours. We do our best when we trust in ourselves and are confident that our intentions and efforts are thoughtful and carefully chosen. And, when discussing family concerns with our spouse, the conversation will be most productive if we can, as consistently as possible, make sure our tone embodies respect and appreciation.

Another area that requires our attention is our social roles—mother, sibling, daughter, friend, wife, volunteer, employee. They all go through different phases with ups and downs. The relationships we have in each of the roles vary in importance to each of us and from time to time, but whatever the level of significance, the communication takes time and energy. And, just as we want to be clear about our feelings and express them succinctly, we need to listen—pay attention to what messages others are giving. We need to pay attention to what their behavior says as well as their words. As the mothers in my study learned about parenting, listening to our children was one of the critical behaviors they learned and valued over time.

One of the major benefits to many of us is the support and validation we feel from some of these relationships—time and energy well spent and very important. Each of us needs validation that we are good people, good mothers, good wives, good employees, or whatever other roles we assume. With this validation we feel good about ourselves and are able to reach out and care for our family. In turn, and with attention to our circumstances and values, we are able to make decisions that are good for our children, our families, and our work status, and create a sense of well-being as adult women.

We can manage. We can balance. We can decide. We can grow our children. We can grow as independent adults. Our efforts are true and honest and we can be proud.

Appendix

Graph 1

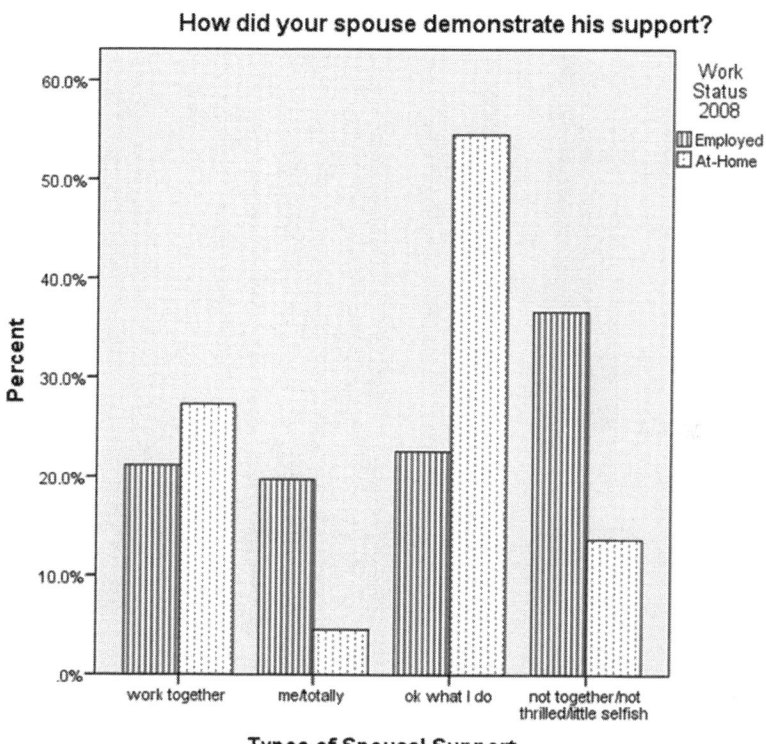

How did your spouse demonstrate his support?

[Bar graph showing Work Status 2008, comparing Employed (stripes) and At-Home (dots) mothers across four categories of spousal support: "work together", "me/totally", "ok what I do", and "not together/not thrilled/little selfish". Y-axis shows Percent from 0% to 60%. X-axis labeled "Types of Spousal Support".]

The graph above compares the amount and kind of support the employed (stripes) and at-home (dots) mothers felt they received from their spouses. The striped bars represent the percent of employed mothers in a category and the dotted bars represent the percent of at-home mothers in a category.

Note that the highest percentage (55%) was of at-home mothers who thought their husbands were okay with their stay-at-home work status. Thirty-seven percent of the employed mothers felt a lack of spousal support because 1) they were either divorced, or 2) their husbands were "not thrilled with my working full time," or 3) "being a little selfish."

Graph 2

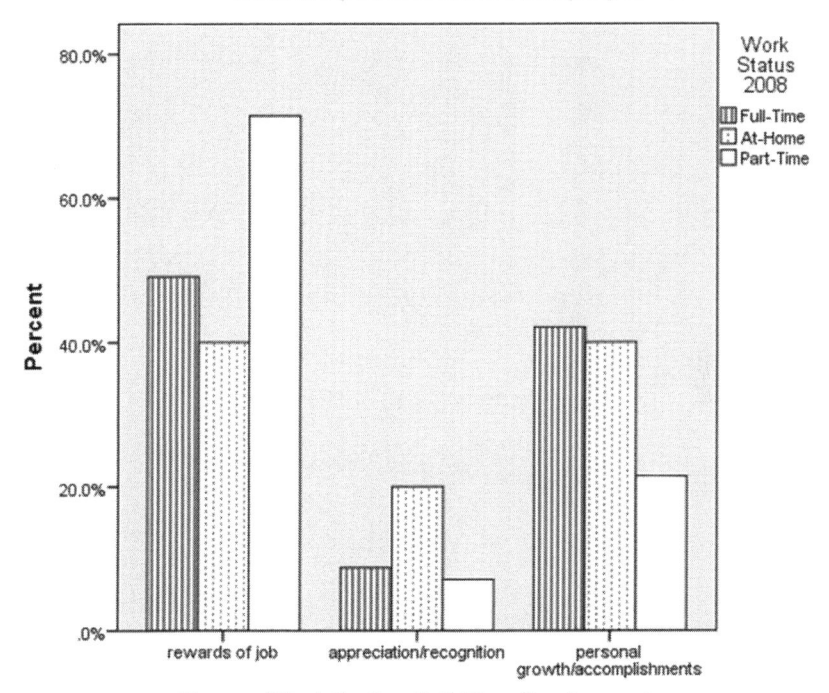

If you ever experienced full-time employment, what did you find most satisfying about it?

Types of Satisfaction Full-Time Employment

Further confirmation that full-time employment has very satisfying rewards is in the graph above. As you can see, the striped bars, representing the full-time employed mothers, are pretty equal above the categories: "rewards of the job" and "personal growth and accomplishments"—49 and 42 percent, respectively. Given that 80 percent of the mothers who were employed full time in 1994 remained in full-time employment in 2008, it is safe to surmise that these tangible rewards and the personal rewards obtained in full-time employment outweigh the frustration and stress experienced by most of these mothers.

Another interesting aspect of the graph is the responses of the part-time employed mothers in 2008 represented by the plain bars. Note that the tallest one, which is above "rewards of the job," represents 71 percent of the part-time employed mothers in 2008—that is a large percent! What is interesting is that 37 percent of these mothers were at home in 1994 compared to the 15 percent who were employed full time in 1994—more than double.

Graph 3

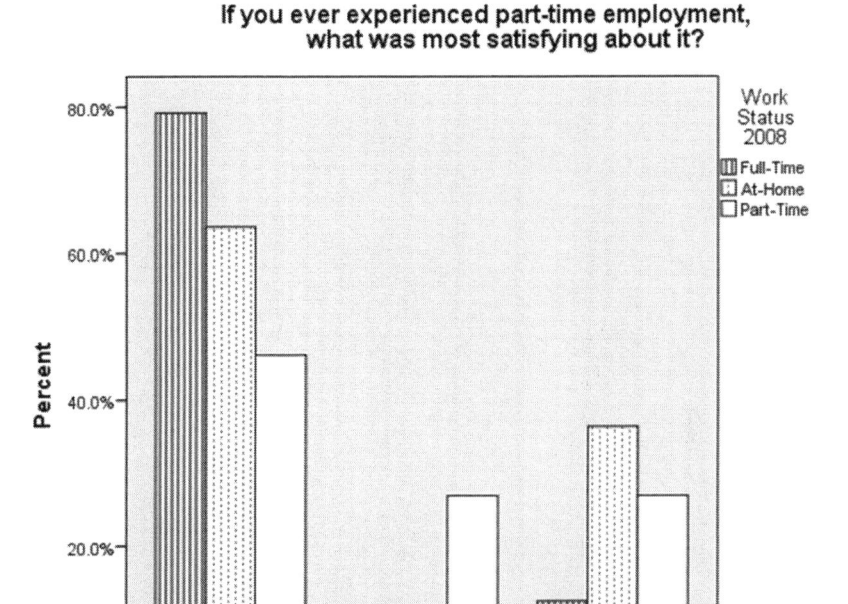

If you ever experienced part-time employment, what was most satisfying about it?

Types of Satisfaction Part-Time Employment

A quick look at this graph shows that the tallest bars in the graph are above the category titled "good balance." This means that all mothers whether they were currently (2008) employed full or part time, or at home with their children, thought part-time employment offered a "good balance." The (79%) of employed full time mothers—denoted by the tallest striped bar—valued "good balance," having less time at the office and more time at home, more than the other work status groups.

Graph 4

If you experienced being at home full time, what was most satisfying about it?

Work Status 1994
- Employed
- At-Home

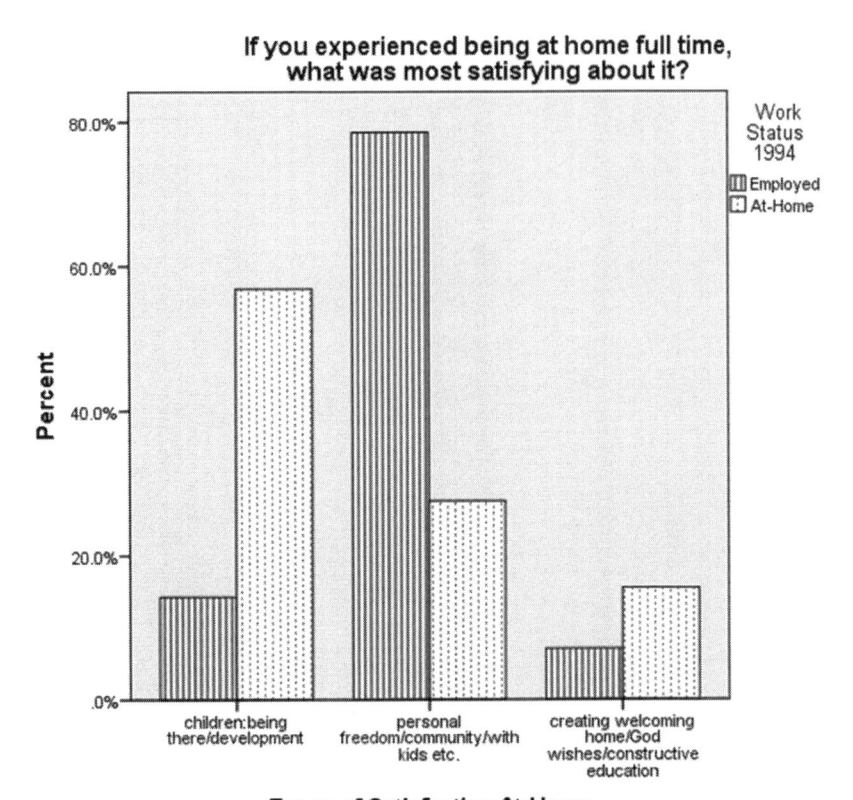

Types of Satisfaction At-Home:
- children: being there/development
- personal freedom/community/with kids etc.
- creating welcoming home/God wishes/constructive education

The graph above shows the percent of mothers— employed and at-home—who cited either development of children, personal freedom, or creating a welcoming home as a source of satisfaction.

Just looking at the striped and dotted bars, you can see that in the original, 1994 study, at-home mothers (dotted) definitely had different sources of satisfaction from the employed mothers (striped). Approximately 57 percent of the mothers who were at home in 1994 found satisfaction from being able to be there for their children and watching and helping with their development.

Graph 5

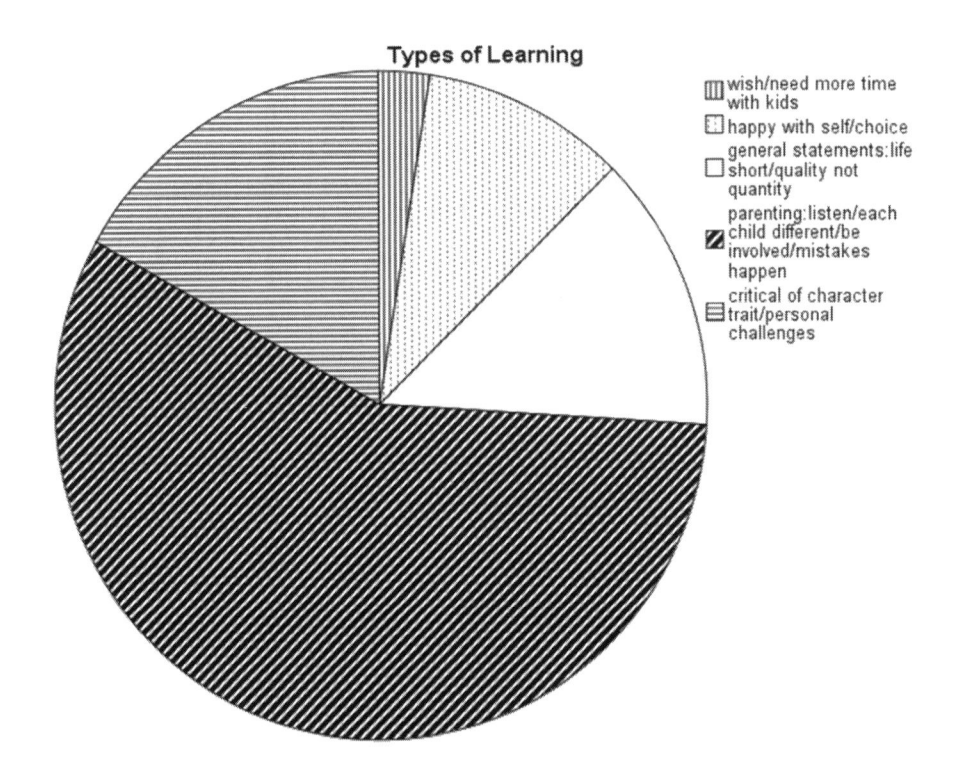

Types of Learning

- wish/need more time with kids
- happy with self/choice
- general statements: life short/quality not quantity
- parenting: listen/each child different/be involved/mistakes happen
- critical of character trait/personal challenges

Looking at the responses of all the mothers—see the dark striped section in the pie chart—most of them (57%) wrote that they learned parenting skills: listen to your children, support them, treat them differently; each child is unique; let them learn from their mistakes. The second highest percent of responses cited by 17 percent of all mothers—see the horizontal striped section of the pie chart—created a category on learning about oneself: I needed more patience; I should have been a better listener; flexibility is important.

Graph 6

How did your work status affect your free time?

Work Status 2008
- Employed
- At-Home

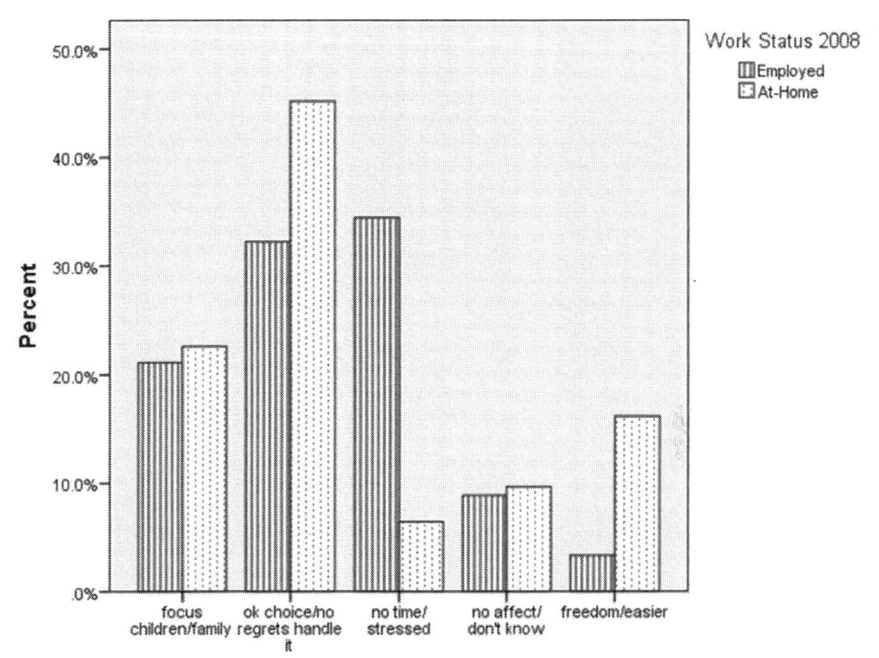

Percent (Y-axis, 0% to 50%)

Categories (X-axis): focus children/family | ok choice/no regrets handle it | no time/ stressed | no affect/ don't know | freedom/easier

Effects of Work Status on Free Time

Looking at this graph you can see that the largest difference between the striped bar— (34%) of the full- and part-time employed mothers, and the dotted bar—(6%) of the at-home mothers in 2008 is the category labeled "no time/stressed." The employed mothers overwhelmingly compared to the mothers at home, are too stressed trying to answer the calls of employment and their own family to have time to readily reach out to friends and other family members— siblings and parents or cousins.

Graph 7

Mothers who were at home full time in 1994

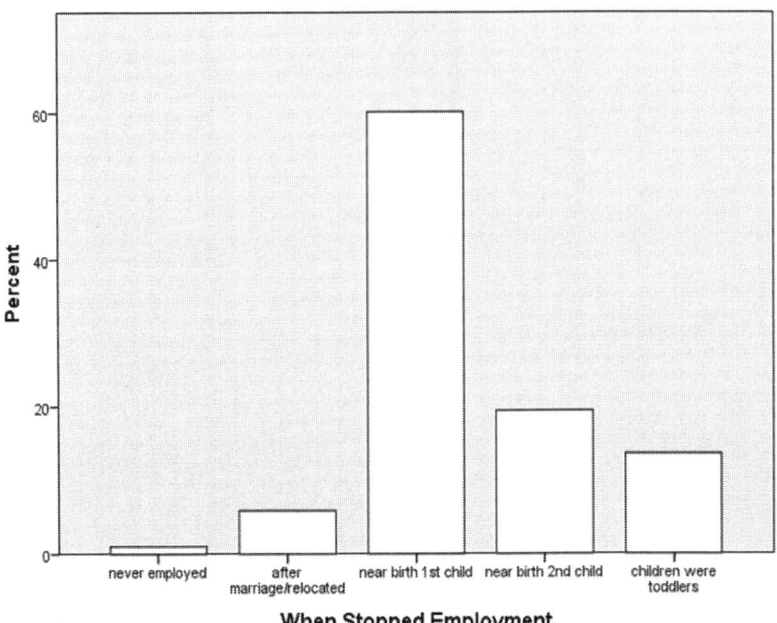

[Bar chart with y-axis "Percent" (0 to 60+) and x-axis "When Stopped Employment" showing categories: never employed (~1%), after marriage/relocated (~6%), near birth 1st child (~60%), near birth 2nd child (~20%), children were toddlers (~14%)]

The graph above shows when these women, who became at-home mothers, stepped out of the workforce. As you can see, the tallest rectangle over "near the birth of 1st child" represents the largest group of mothers (60%) who stopped employment to stay home. Some mothers plan on staying home before they become pregnant. Others find they just cannot leave their baby with someone else, and others realize it doesn't make sense to return to employment because their salary will all go to childcare—what is the benefit?

Graph 8

Mothers who were employed full time in 1994

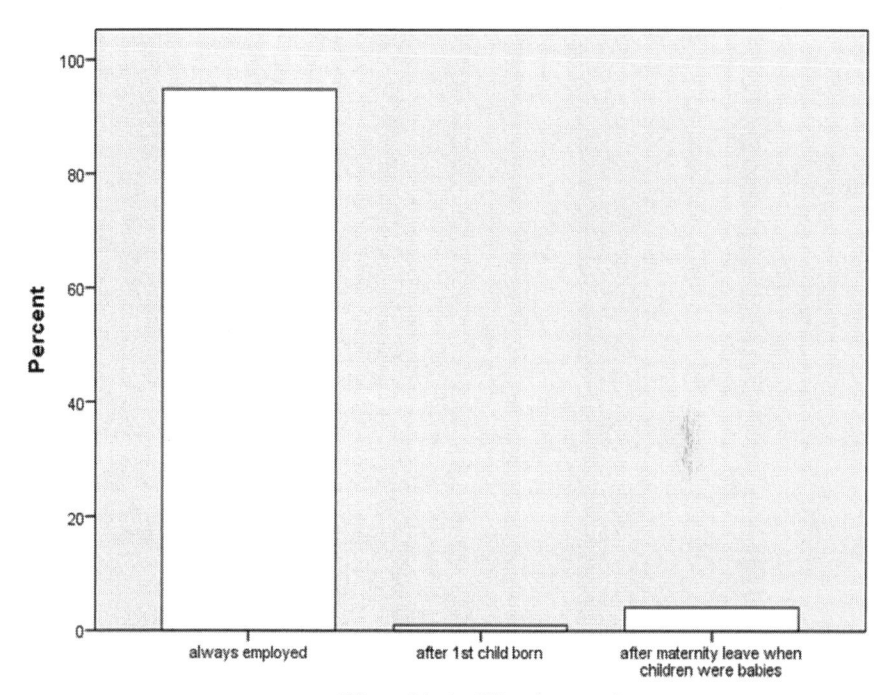

[Bar chart showing Percent vs. When Started Employment: "always employed" ~95%, "after 1st child born" ~1%, "after maternity leave when children were babies" ~3%]

Looking at this graph, which represents the employed mothers in my 1994 study, one sees that almost all of them (95%) maintained employment. Probably most of the full-time employed mothers took the maternity leave allotted by their employer but they generally did not extend their time home.

Graph 9

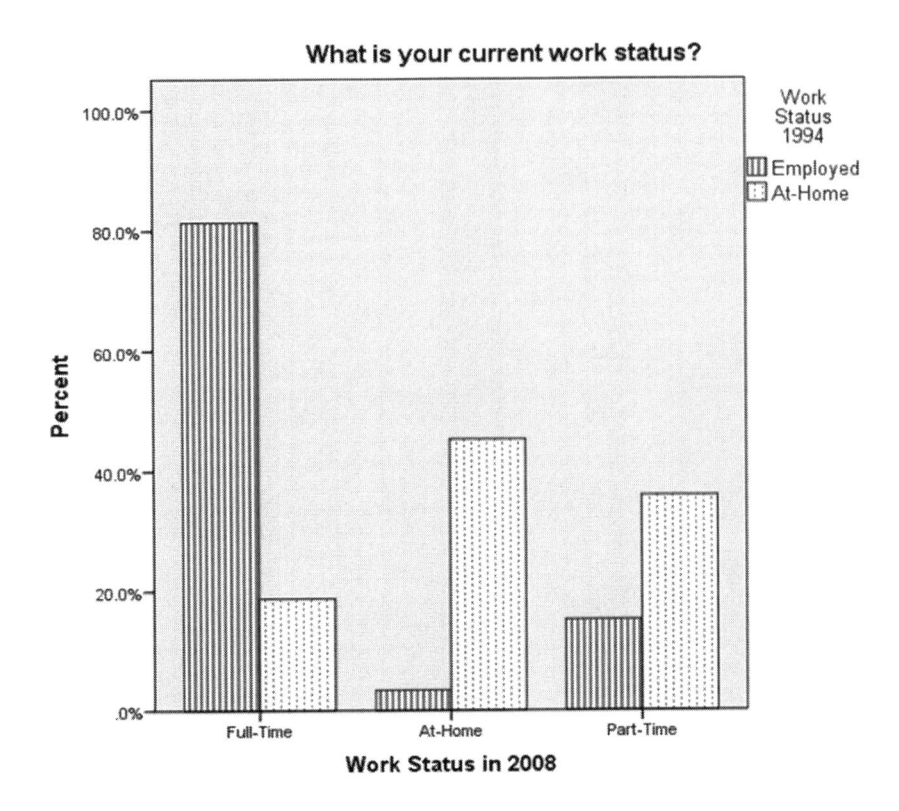

What is your current work status?

[Bar chart showing Work Status in 2008 (Full-Time, At-Home, Part-Time) broken down by Work Status 1994 (Employed, At-Home). Y-axis: Percent, 0% to 100%. Full-Time: Employed ~82%, At-Home ~19%. At-Home: Employed ~3%, At-Home ~46%. Part-Time: Employed ~16%, At-Home ~36%.]

These mothers were relatively consistent about maintaining employment. This graph depicts the work status in 2008 of the originally employed and at-home mothers in 1994. You can see that 80 percent of the mothers who were employed full time in 1994—the tallest striped bar—were employed full time fourteen years later, in 2008.

Graph 10

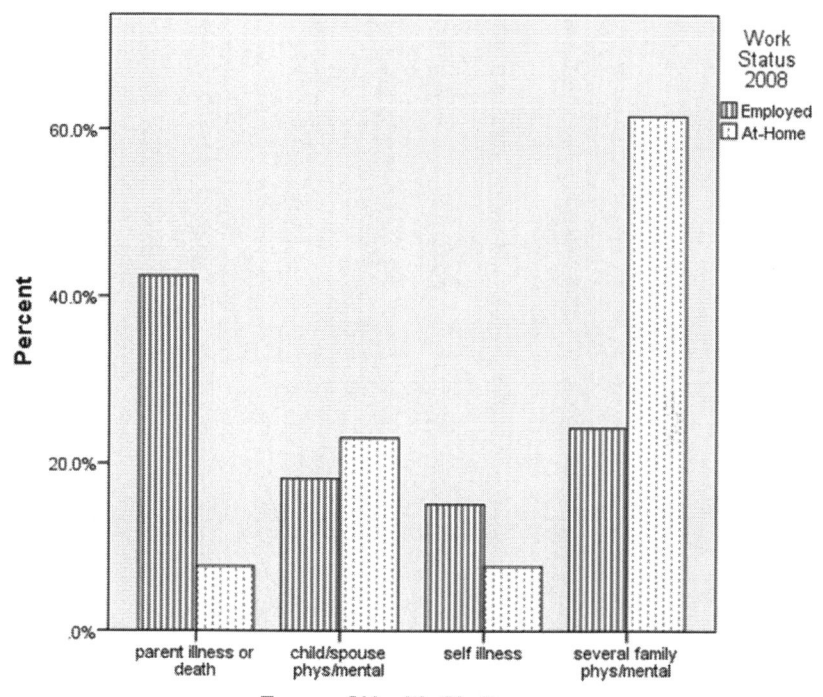

Have you experienced significant challenges/stresses over the past fourteen years?

[Bar graph showing Types of Health Challenges by Work Status 2008 (Employed vs. At-Home). Categories: parent illness or death, child/spouse phys/mental, self illness, several family phys/mental. Y-axis: Percent.]

The graph above compares the percent of employed mothers with the at-home mothers in the health-problem categories. The highest bar (62%) on the graph—dotted—for at-home mothers in 2008, is above the category indicating that several family members had physical or mental health problems. The second highest bar (42%)—striped—for employed mothers in 2008, is above the category marked parent illness or death. When I examined the responses closely, I found that many of the "several family members" included parental illness and/or death. The takeaway from this graph is that as we and our children grow, our parents age too.

Graph 11a

Are any of your children challenged by learning disabilities?

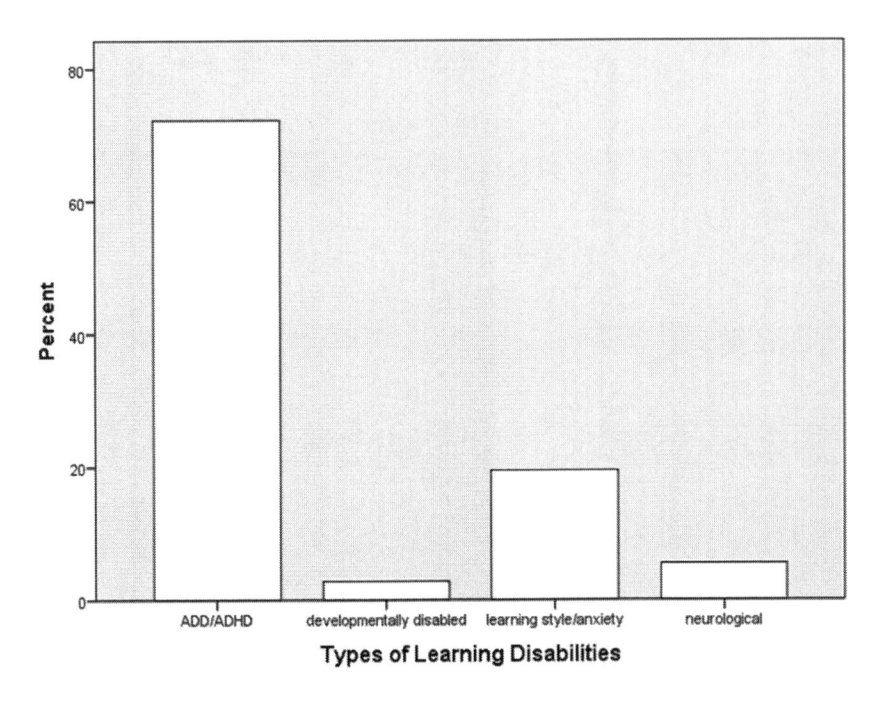

[Bar chart showing Percent on y-axis (0-80) versus Types of Learning Disabilities on x-axis: ADD/ADHD (~72%), developmentally disabled (~3%), learning style/anxiety (~20%), neurological (~5%)]

Types of Learning Disabilities

Graph 11a shows that of the mothers who reported their children have learning challenges, 72 percent of them cited ADD/ADHD. The percent of children from my study (8.2%) is pretty consistent with the national statistic of 9% mentioned in the above report.

Graph 11b

Are any of your children challenged by learning disabilities?

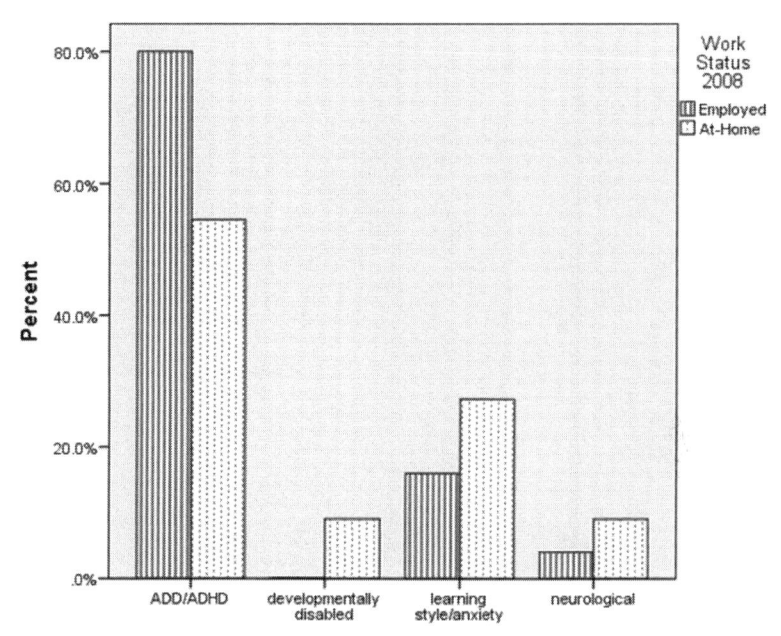

[Bar chart showing percentages by Work Status 2008 (Employed vs At-Home) across types of learning disabilities: ADD/ADHD, developmentally disabled, learning style/anxiety, neurological]

Types of Learning Disabilities

An examination of Graph 11b compares the percent of employed mothers in 2008 with at-home mothers who have children with ADHD. It is interesting to see that 80 percent of the employed mothers—represented by the tallest striped bar—compared to 55 percent of the at-home mothers—represented by tallest dotted bar—have children diagnosed with attentiveness learning challenges. Why are 25 percent more of employed mothers reporting children with ADHD?

Graph 12

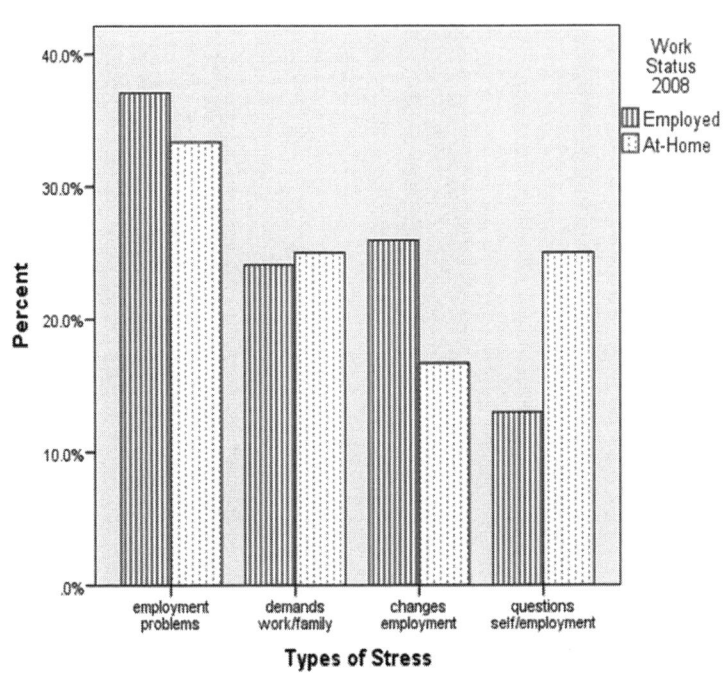

Was there any conflict or stress specifically related to a work status since 1994?

Types of Stress

The responses of the work status groups represented in this graph by the taller dotted bar—at-home mothers (25%), and the striped bar—employed mothers (13%) above the category "questions about self/employment" illustrate some of the more personal situations that can cause stress for mothers. The quotes contain feelings of inadequacy that we women recognize and sometimes admit we have. In any case, these feelings do not make us feel good and take up energy so we have less to give to others—starting with our children.

Graph 13

What circumstances best utilize your qualities and abilities?

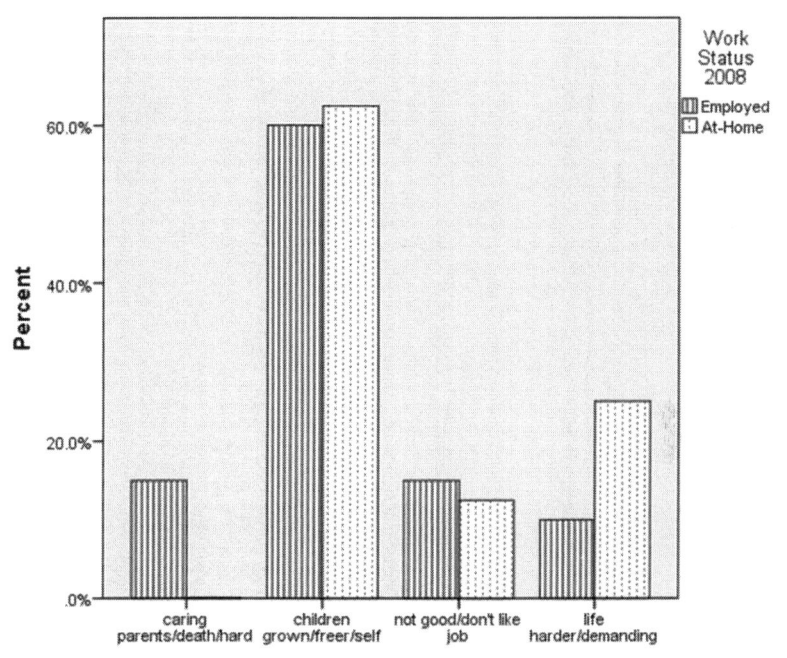

[Bar graph showing Work Status 2008 (Employed vs At-Home) across categories: caring parents/death/hard; children grown/freer/self; not good/don't like job; life harder/demanding]

Categories that utilize Qualities and Abilities

The graph above depicts the categories the mothers thought brought out their best qualities and abilities in any role. As you can see, according to the mothers, launching your children can be a very positive experience. The tallest striped bar which represents 60 percent of the employed mothers, and the tallest dotted bar, which represents 63 percent of the at-home mothers in 2008 is above the category labeled "children grown/freer/self"—in other words, after their children left the home, they felt freer in the role of mother to expand their own interests and were better able to use their capabilities.

Graph 14

What are you proudest about yourself as a person?

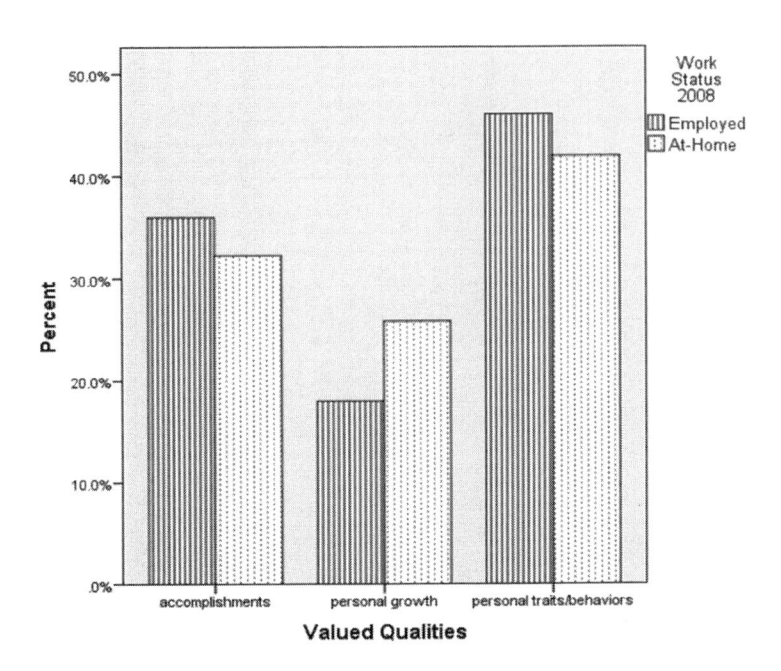

As you can see in the graph above, the employed mothers (46%)—the highest striped bar, only slightly more than the at-home mothers, (42%)—the highest dotted bar—cited their personal traits and behaviors as the qualities for which they were most proud.

Graph 15

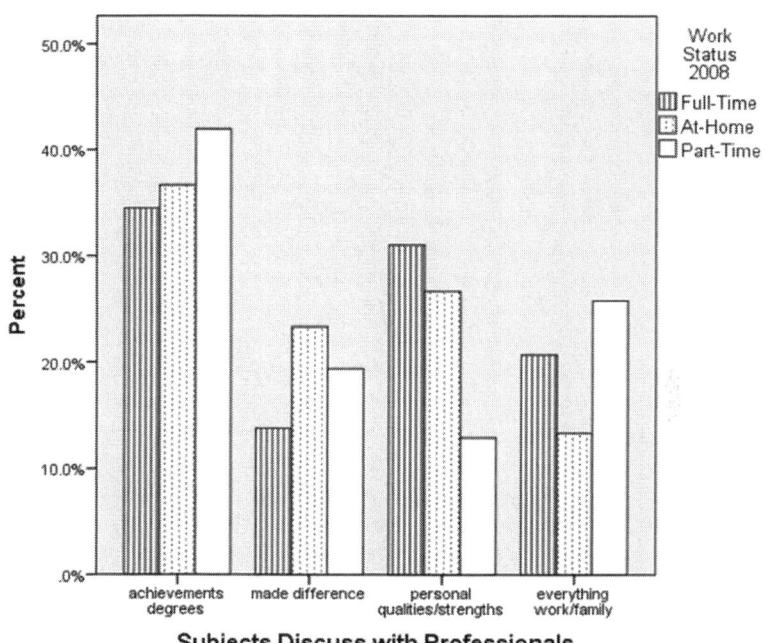

If you were talking with professionals, what would you want them to know about you?

The above graph shows once again that predominantly all the work status groups employed full time (35%)—represented by the tallest striped bar, part time (42%)—represented by the tallest white bar, and at-home mothers (37%) represented by the tallest dotted bar, would talk about the same subjects: achievements, degrees, and titles, when talking with a group of professionals.

Graph 16

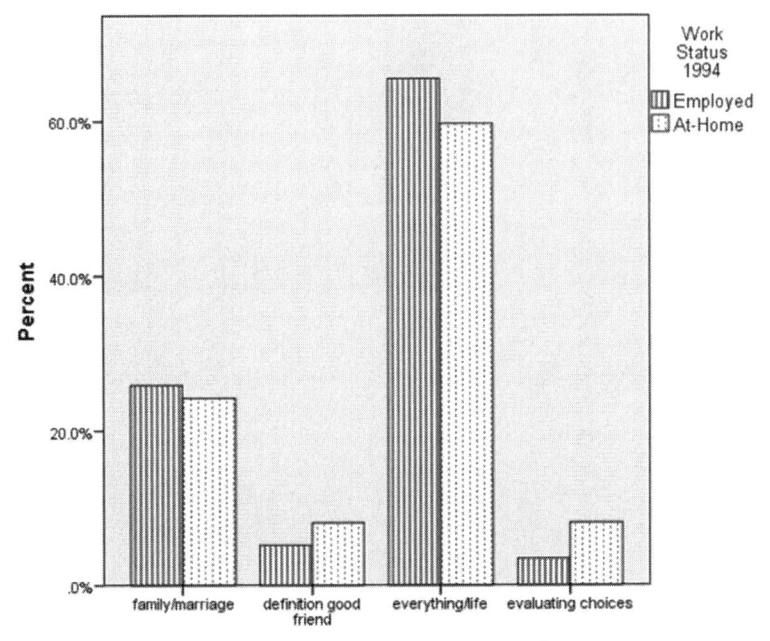

If you were talking with an old friend, what would you want them to know about you?

Subjects Discuss with Old Friends

As the graph above depicts, 66 percent of mothers who were employed in 1994—represented by the tallest striped bar—and 59 percent of the mothers who were at home in 1994—represented by the tallest dotted bar—noted that they would talk about everything—personal life, work, hopes, to longtime friends. This trend held true in an examination of the 2008 work status groups. The full-time employed (61%), part-time employed (53%), and at-home mothers (74%)—the highest percent in each work status group—cited they would talk about everything to an old friend.

Graph 17

Over the past thirteen years, how has your spouse demonstrated his support or lack of support for your work status?

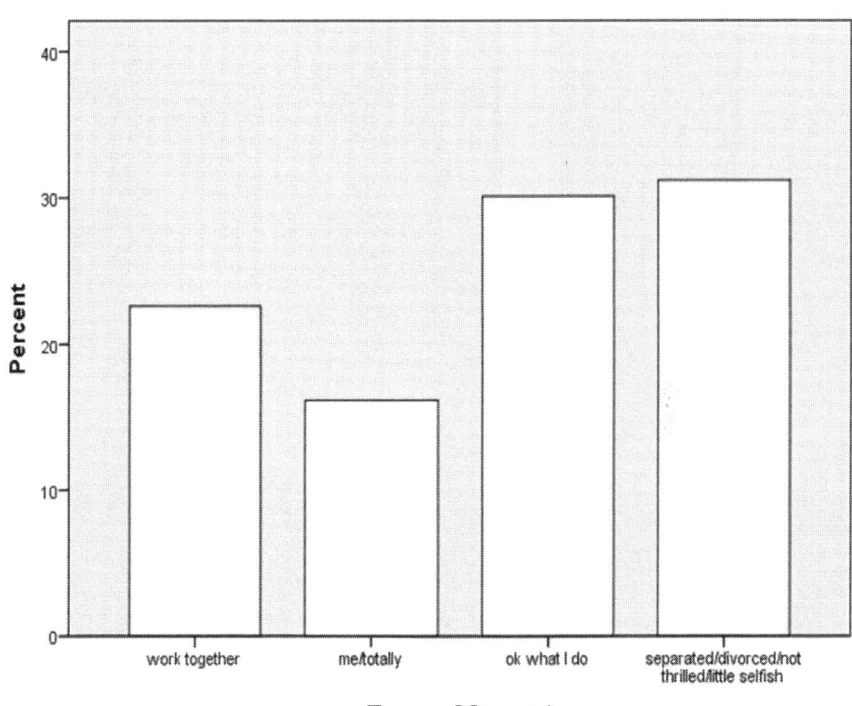

[Bar chart with y-axis "Percent" (0-40) and x-axis "Types of Support" showing four bars: "work together" (~23%), "me/totally" (~16%), "ok what I do" (~30%), "separated/divorced/not thrilled/little selfish" (~31%)]

This chart illustrates spousal support across all work statuses. Most of the mothers in the study, 88 percent, responded that their spouse was supportive of their work status. But, when the mothers were asked how their spouse demonstrated support over the years, 32 percent of the mothers—the largest category albeit by a small margin—depicted in this graph by the tallest bar, described a lack of support: "we are separated/divorced"; "my spouse isn't thrilled with my work status" or "my spouse is a little selfish—doesn't seem to value all that I do." Why the discrepancy? Why would 88 percent say their husbands were supportive but then a third of them write that in retrospect, they were not supportive? Could it be that initially or for a long period their spouse was supportive, but looking at the dynamics now, he could improve…?

Graph 18

Was your spouse supportive of your work status?

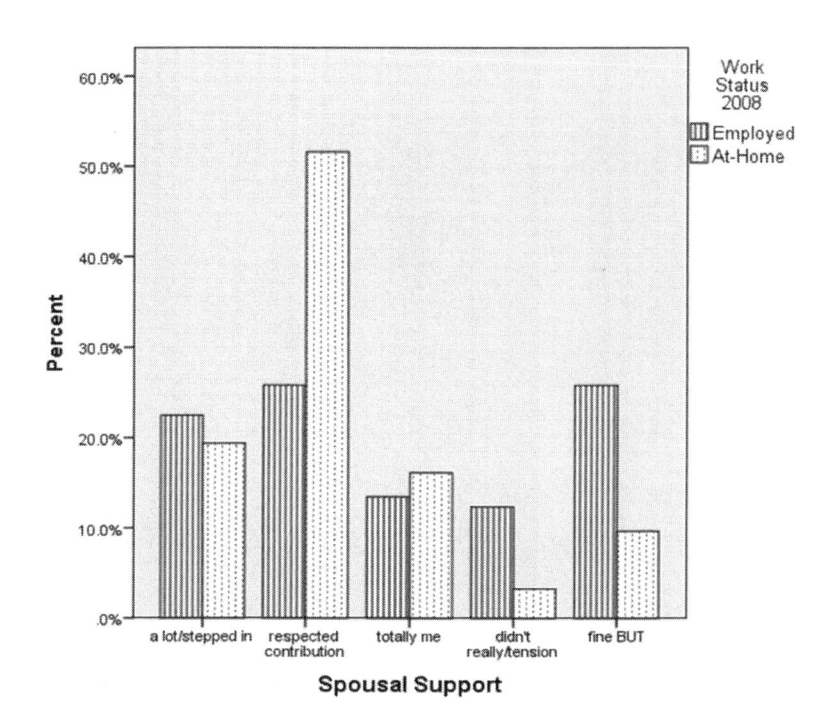

(Bar chart showing Percent vs. Spousal Support categories: "a lot/stepped in", "respected contribution", "totally me", "didn't really/tension", "fine BUT", grouped by Work Status 2008: Employed and At-Home)

As you can see in this graph, by far, most (52%) of the mothers—represented by the tallest dotted bar—were at home in 2008 above the category "respected contribution." In 2008, 26 percent of the employed mothers were evenly split—represented by the two tallest striped bars, that identified spousal support, the first above the category "respect for contribution," the second above the category "fine BUT."

Graph 19

Were your friends supportive of your work status?

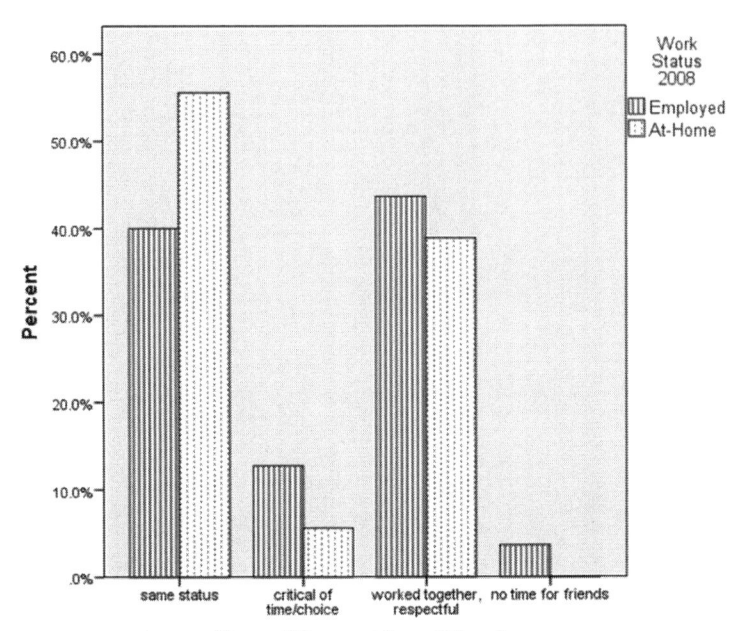

[Bar chart showing Percent (0% to 60%) vs Type of Support from Friends, with categories: same status, critical of time/choice, worked together/respectful, no time for friends. Work Status 2008: Employed (striped) and At-Home (dotted).]

Type of Support from Friends

This graph reveals an interesting comparison of the types of support the mothers received from friends. While both groups had high percentages in the categories "same status" and "worked together," they differed in degree on the type of support friends gave. The highest percentage of at-home mothers (56%)—represented by the tallest dotted bar—were in the category "same work status": their friends from whom they gained support were also at home. The highest percentage (47%) of employed mothers—represented by the tallest striped bar—were in the category "worked together."

Graph 20

Were your children supportive of your work status?

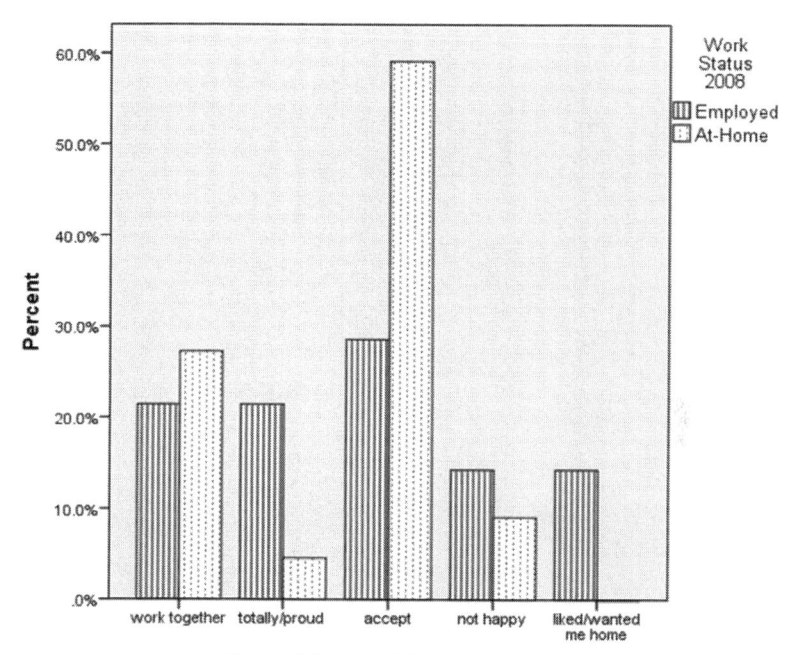

Type of Support from Children

The largest dotted bar (59%) in this chart, which represents the at-home mothers in 2008, is above the category "accepts." Translation: the children see their mother as doing what mothers are expected to do—take care of children. No big deal, nothing exciting, just what is expected. However, the percentage of employed mothers was higher than at-home mothers on three other types of support they received from their children:

1) 21 percent "totally/proud." These mothers proudly reiterated the respectful and inquiring support they

received from their children who were eager to learn about them and their employment.

2) 14 percent of employed and no at-home mothers commented that the children "liked/wanted me home."

3) 14 percent of employed and 9 percent of at-home mothers were in the category "not happy." Do you think it is possible the children of employed mothers are playing into their mothers' vulnerability to feel guilty about "not always being available, i.e., not being home?"

Graph 21

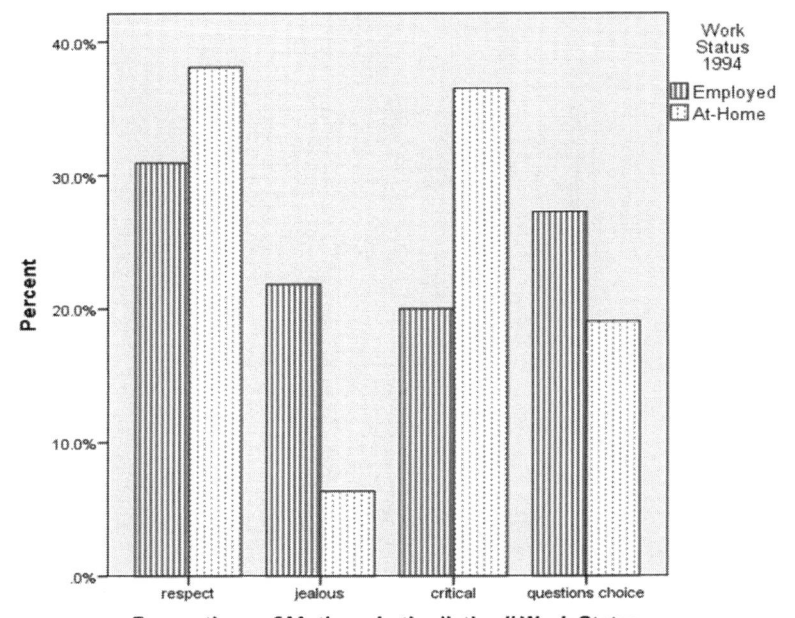

In 1994, what were your thoughts/perceptions of mothers who chose a different work status from you?

[Bar graph showing percentages for Employed (striped) and At-Home (dotted) mothers across four categories: respect, jealous, critical, questions choice]

Perceptions of Mothers in the "other" Work Status

The employed mothers, depicted by the striped bars, do not strongly group above any particular category—ranging from 31 percent writing about respect, to 27 percent regarding comments that question their choices, to 21 percent "feeling jealous," to 20 percent conveying criticism. On the other hand, the dotted bars that represent the at-home mothers in 1994 have two prominent categories that emerge: 38 percent expressing respect for employed mothers and 37 percent expressing criticism of employed mothers. The mothers who were at-home in 1994 seem to have distinct and dichotomous feelings about employed mothers when their children were young.

Graph 22

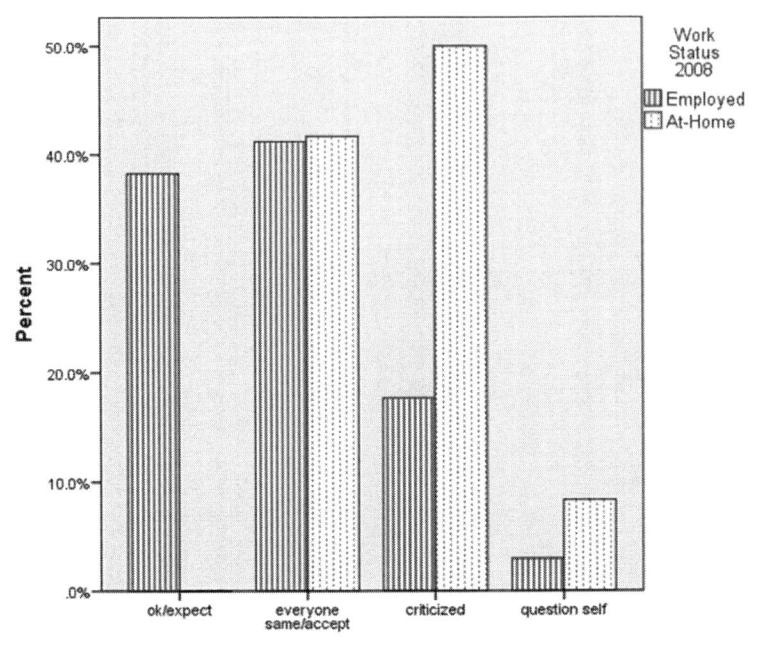

Did the social reaction you received regarding your work status change as your children got older?

Percent vs **Types of Reactions in Social Situations** (ok/expect, everyone same/accept, criticized, question self), grouped by Work Status 2008: Employed, At-Home.

The "Types of Reactions to Social Situations" graph above representing the categories that emerged from the comments of employed and at-home mothers conveys a wonderful picture of the change in reaction to social situations when the at-home mothers became employed. Is one reason for this new reaction because society's mantra, "a mother belongs in the home," no longer has the same impact when the children are launched or at minimum, no longer babies? Or, is society's critical mantra about employed mothers really, "a mother of babies and toddlers belongs at home?"

You will notice that not one at-home mother in 2008—no dotted bar—wrote that the reaction they received in social situations about their work status was "ok/expect." This is because they were not doing what was expected now that the children were older. They were expected not to remain at home. To support this social reaction is the largest dotted bar (50%) of the at-home mothers above the category "criticized." It seems that society now has a different mantra for at-home mothers too: if a mother no longer has very young children she belongs in the workforce!

Graph 23

What was your experience with the teachers, principal or other parents when at your child's school?

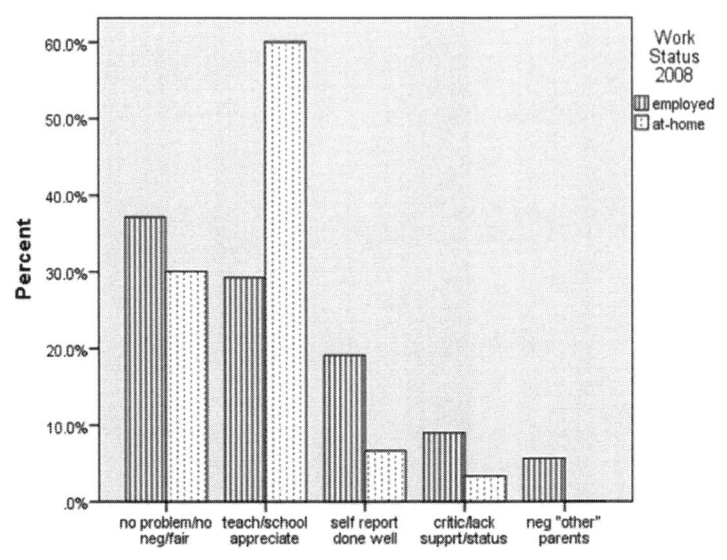

[Bar graph showing percentages by Work Status 2008 (employed vs. at-home) across types of reactions from teachers/school officials: no problem/no neg/fair; teach/school appreciate; self report done well; critic/lack supprt/status; neg "other" parents]

Types of Reactions from Teachers/School Officials

Looking at this 2008 work status graph, you can see that reflecting back to when their children were young, the at-home mothers (60%)—the tallest dotted bar—felt appreciated compared to a smaller percentage of the employed mothers (29%). Slightly more of the employed mothers (37%) than the at-home mothers (30%) perceived no problems at all. And, 6 percent of employed mothers compared to none of at-home mothers felt "negative" reactions from mothers in the "other" work status.

Graph 24

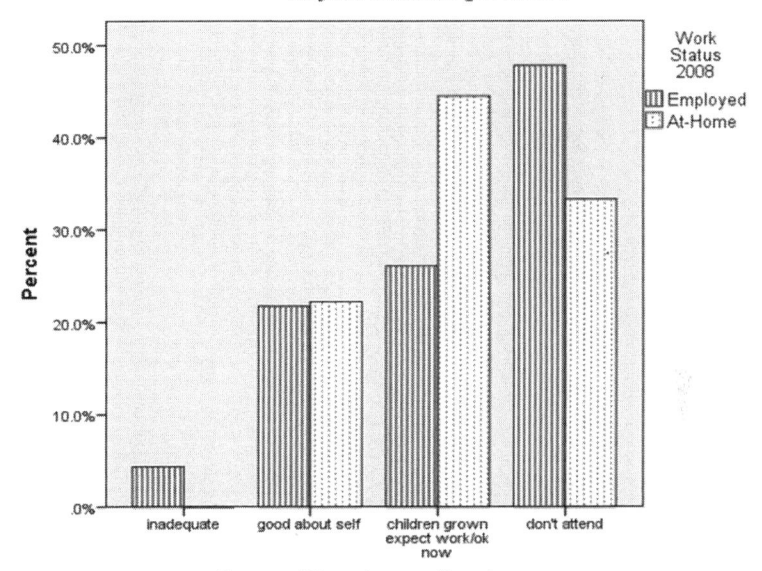

Did the reaction at reunions regarding your work status change as your children got older?

[Bar chart showing Types of Reactions at Reunions by Work Status 2008 (Employed vs At-Home), Y-axis: Percent 0.0% to 50.0%. Categories: inadequate, good about self, children grown expect work/ok now, don't attend]

Types of Reactions at Reunions

This graph depicts the percentage of each mother group that chose to write about one of the categories. Most of the employed mothers in 2008 (48%)—represented by the tallest striped bar—were primarily the group that did not attend reunions. Whether or not the employed mothers become busier and have more demands on them when the children are older, it is hard to say, but these comments are typical: "I have had no time to attend reunions"; "Didn't go—too busy working."

The at-home mothers in 2008 (44%)—represented by the tallest dotted bar—found that people's reactions at reunions were similar to their reactions in social situations and at their children's schools. But unlike the previous reasons—their children are older and the mothers are "expected to work," these mothers have grown to be comfortable with their work status of not being employed and more confidently can say that and be accepted by their friends.

Acknowledgments

The Roads Taken would not have been possible without the generosity of the 200 mothers who agreed to participate in my dissertation research in 1994. Particularly when their only reward for finding time between employment or caring for at least one young— preschool child— and home responsibilities was a packet of flavored instant International coffee to drink while filling out my questionnaires. And, I am forever grateful to the incredible 123 of these same mothers who answered a myriad of questions about their experiences as employed or at-home mothers fourteen years later. Their heartfelt, honest, and thoughtful responses drove the topics and discussions in this book. If but for the promise of anonymity, I would gladly name and praise each of them for not only sharing about their efforts to help their children reach their goals but also, helping me, who they didn't even know, fulfill my goal.

Next I thank Janet Heddesheimer, Ph.D., my dissertation advisor and over the years, wise counsel and good friend, always supporting and creatively questioning my research interests. Without her patience, insight, and guidance, I never would have completed my dissertation.

Speaking of patience and guidance, I thank Donna Cedar-Southworth who helped me find my voice, a huge accomplishment! I had several false starts with editors who were taking me in directions that became uncomfortable. Donna "got" my research and in an incredibly positive way encouraged me to keep writing until my voice was no longer academic and I could "share" my information, ideas, and myself.

Obviously, without the interest and support of my publisher, Nell Minow, I wouldn't have a book. Thank you, Nell, for deciding to make niche books available to the public and giving me the opportunity to be one you selected. I consider myself extremely lucky to be working with you. And, thank you, Nell, for introducing me to your editor, Deborah Davidson, who is not only a delightful and interesting person but also an excellent editor. Her experience, keen eye, and intelligence "cleaned up" my manuscript so that readers will join me in being forever grateful for her careful attention to the content, presentation, and grammar in *The Roads Taken*.

I also thank Kristen Skelton, a mother of three young ones in the midst of deciding about employment versus staying home, who mentioned that she had gone to the library to search for answers. I told her to "stop right there" and asked if she would read my unedited manuscript and give me feedback. If she ever decides she wants part-time employment she too could become an editor. I am so grateful for her insightful comments; sharing new ways of looking at situations once she read my manuscript; and regretting that I did not tell her what to do, realized that I gave her the tools. There was and is no way that I could speak for her intelligent and aware self; it is her life, her decision; she knows best.

I also am very grateful to my friends and acquaintances who offered to read sections and share their impressions which definitely made me think and rethink my work: Susan Armstrong, Judy Bailey, Vicky Chiang, Suzy Cramer, Lindsay Garland, Helen Haltzel, Jean

Hannon, Nancy Keener, Beth Stroul, Kaye Taylor, Peggy Taylor, and Robin Westbrook.

I am equally thankful to my longtime friends who consistently supported my efforts, always asking and encouraging me to continue and sometimes helping me sort out ideas: Janet Barsy, Megan Beyer, Miriam Coffman, Marty McGrane, Julie Osherson, Marjorie Rosenberg, Sherrill Wells, and my wonderful sister, Linda Green. A new and very special friend, my daughter-in-law, Hannah Farber, always encouraged me to write, write, write, as she too was avoiding writing... her dissertation. And, if I sent her something to read, her comments were always substantive, most intelligent, and supportive. Thank you, Hannah! (I am one lucky mother-in-law.)

I was unable to get answers to problems I had with the software—Statistical Package for Social Science (SPSS)—I used to create my beautiful graphs until I spoke with Robert (Bob) Gluting, a marketing manager. He called me to discuss my business account. Although he soon learned I was not a business but a lone user of the software, he went way beyond his job description to find the answers I needed. People who go out of their way to help are rare and wonderful; Bob is one of those people.

In addition I thank two people who gave time and support educating me how to write a proposal and navigate the publishing world: Lynne Olson, author of *Citizens of London*, and Robin Gradison, TV news producer.

Finally, I thank my family obviously because they have afforded me the pleasure of being their mother or in the case of my husband, his wife. They have each added so much to my life—experiences, education, and love—extraordinary. Focusing on *The*

Roads Taken, I thank my son, Derek Miller, who early on read startup drafts with a kind, most encouraging and incredibly intelligent eye; my daughter, Alexis Miller, who, always my wonderful cheerleader and compatriot, articulated fabulous ideas and creative ways for me to proceed; and my husband, Harris Miller, who more than tolerated my many interruptions when a thought—however minor—occurred to me, helped me sort out points of confusion, and always always was my greatest advocate.

Bibliography

Baumrind, D. (1967). Child care practices anteceding three patterns of preschool behavior. *Genetic Psychology Monographs,* 75(1), 43-88.

"British women are wasting their education by becoming stay-at-home mothers." A Prime Minister of Denmark, Helle Thorning-Schmidt. http://www.dailymail.co.uk/femail/article-2115170/Can-woman-clever-stay-home-mum.html#ixzz2ck7xwJ1L

Clinton, Hillary. *It Takes a Village: And Other Lessons Our Children Teach Us.* New York: Simon and Shuster, 1996.

Crittenden, Ann. *The Price of Motherhood: Why the Most Important Job in the World Is Still the Least Valued.* New York: Metropolitan Books, 2001.

-- *If You've Raised a Kid, You Can Manage Anything: Leadership Begins At Home.* New York: Gotham, 2004.

Crosby, Faye. *Juggling: The Unexpected Advantage of Balancing Career and Home for Women and Their Families.* New York: Free Press, 1991.

"Increasing Prevalence of Parent-Reported Attention-Deficit/Hyperactivity Disorder Among Children—

United States, 2003 and 2007." Center for Disease Control and Prevention report. (2010) http://www.cdc.gov/mmwr/preview/mmwrhtml/mm5944a3.htm

Maccoby, E.E. and J.A. Martin. (1983). "Socialization in the context of the family: Parent–child interaction." In P. Mussen and E.M. Hetherington, editors, *Handbook of Child Psychology*, Volume IV: "Socialization, personality, and social development." New York: Wiley, 4th edition.

Mason, Mary Ann and Eve Mason Ekman. *Mothers on the Fast Track: How a Generation Can Balance Family and Careers*, New York: Oxford University Press, 2008.

Meers, Sharon and Joanna Strober. *Getting to 50/50: How Couples Can Have It All by Sharing It All.* New York: Bantam, 2009.

Miller, Jean Baker. *Toward a New Psychology of Women.* Boston: Beacon Press, 1976/1986.

Milne, A.A. *Winnie-The-Pooh.* New York: E.P. Dutton, 1926.

Morgan, O. and K. Skelton (2014). "The Shriver Report: A woman's nation pushes back from the brink." A Study by Maria Shriver and the Center for American Progress.

Powell, Colin. *It Worked for Me: In Life and Leadership.* New York: Harper, 2012.

Shipler, David. *The Working Poor: Invisible in America.* New York: Vintage, 2004/2005.

Slaughter, Anne-Marie. "Why Women Still Can't Have it All." http://www.theatlantic.com/magazine/archive/2012/07/why-women-still-cant-have-it-all/309020.

Wang, W., K. Parker, and P. Taylor. "Breadwinner Moms: Mothers Are the Sole or Primary Provider in Four-in-Ten Households with Children; Public Conflicted about the Growing Trend." http://www.pewsocialtrends.org/2013/05/29/breadwinner-moms/.

Working Mother Statistics. Source: Pew Research Center, U.S. Bureau of Labor, *Harvard Business Review*, Research Date: 9.11.2012. http://www.statisticbrain.com/working-mother-statistics/.

Miniver Press is a publisher of lively and informative ebooks and print books, available on Amazon, through bookstores, and at miniverpress.com.
Contact the author with any questions or comments at Deborah@theroadstaken.net

Made in the USA
Middletown, DE
21 December 2014